Best Wishes on your
Birthday - July 1991.
Love Viv.

# Three's Company

# Three's Company

## A Collection of Stories from Aberdeen

By Three Leading Writers

Sheena Blackhall, Rosemary Mackay, Wilma Murray

Selected and introduced by Jessie Kesson

Keith Murray Publications

Published by
Keith Murray Publications
46 Portal Crescent
Tillydrone
Aberdeen
AB2 2SP
Scotland


Printed by Astra Printing Services, Jopps Lane, Aberdeen

ISBN 1 870978 15 3

## ACKNOWLEDGEMENTS

A number of the stories in this volume first appeared in the following publications:

The Wedding Day, Original Prints 3
A Story Without Sense, Original Prints 2
In Exile From Hirta, Cencrastus
Old Wives' Tales, Original Prints 2
Widows' Walk, Scottish Review
The Road to Bernera, New Edinburgh Review
The Kite, New Writing Scotland 2
The Conveyor Belt, Chapman
The Roup, The Buchan Observer
The Swinging Sixties, The Edinburgh Review

Sheena Blackhall's poetry collections to date are:

The Cyard's Kist, published in 1984
The Spik o' the Lan, published in 1986
Hamedrauchtit, published in 1987
Nor' East Neuk, published in 1989
A Nippick o' Nor' East Tales, published in 1989 ( A collection of short stories)
Her latest collection of poetry, Fite Doo  Black Crow is due to be published in 1989

# INTRODUCTION

I was pleased - but apprehensive - when asked to make a selection from the Short Stories of three writers who live and work in Aberdeen.

Pleased, because my "Prentice" years as a writer began in Aberdeen. "Nursed" and encouraged by the Editors of a small, monthly magazine, *North East Review*.

Apprehensive, because I'm not sure that creative writers are the best judges of *other* creative writers. The tendency is to visualise the stories under consideration as you, yourself, would have written them. Particularly when the themes are *known* to you, and with which you have empathy.

Happily - and to my relief - although acquainted with the backgrounds of the stories in *Three's Company* I had no feelings of apprehension. The writers also knew their subjects, and I could not have bettered their interpretations.

"A good Beginning. A strong Ending. And you can sag in the Middle" was how my Dominie at school defined the essentials of a good "Composition". That, I feel, may apply to Novels. But Short Stories need a Flaubertian quality of getting into the guts of a story in few words. And, having got into the guts, keep the tempo going.

In *The Conveyor Belt* Sheena Blackhall achieves that . . . 'Sallie Dempster looked and felt like a camel which had swallowed its hump as her father handed her over to the granite Reception Block of the City's Maternity Hospital . . .'

In this story she takes a belaboured Mother-To-Be through the machine-like processes of modern birth. Leaving mothers like myself of a much older generation, thankful, that in *our* time, birth was a simpler homelier affair.

The local Midwife taking an objective stance, removing herself to warm her backside at the fire in the grate of the bedroom, calmly advising us to . . . "*Push!* And Get ON with it!*" There was a feeling of safety in familiar surroundings, and in the Midwife's matter of fact approach.

In *Tongs Rules OK* a man about to retire to an - "imagined" - life of quiet, suburban ease after bedevilled years of teaching in a school on a Council Estate. Thankful to be leaving . . . 'The windy annex where he worked was a daily tussle with poverty and ignorance. The classroom violence left him physically drained . . . Graffiti screamed down old warnings, old hatreds . . .'

*The Swinging Sixties*. A young girl looking forward to her First Dance may not seem a very *original* theme for a short story. But added to her anticipation of First Time is a terrific desire to be . . . "With It" . . . The first of the . . . PUNKS? . . . No easy achievement in a part of rural Scotland where Change "comes dropping slow". Where . . .

'Calvin still reigns supreme . . .'

And the girl's mother is convinced that . . .

'The swinging sixties were grand for a few painted trollops in London. An actress in Soho could drop as many 'Love Children' as she liked. In Annie's village, they kenned a bastard when they saw it'.

A powerful writer, Sheena Blackhall. I first came to know her work through her poetry. It is the poet in her that gives her writing an extra dimension.

*Letting Go* by Rosemary Mackay is an insight into another aspect of racialism. Unique in that it is not Race against Race but Scot against Scot. A racialism which has always existed between small fishing communities and those whose way of life lies outwith it.

. . . 'They had taught her early that there was more to inclusion in their ranks than marrying one of their sons . . .'

The "Incomer" to a fishing township has a double disadvantage. Another example of racialism. Difference of religion.

'. . . Not for *her* the blacks and muted greys of the Kirk. The marching tunes called hymns. Her faith was rooted in the Roman Catholic way of making beautiful all that they held in reverence . . .'

An insight moving and vivid.

A school girl's "Crush" on "Sir" is an ordinary occurrence. It is when Teacher is "Miss", and herself responds and becomes emotionally involved that *both* become vulnerable to . . . 'The slings and arrows'. . . A vulnerability revealed in Rosemary's story *Down* with a small, distinct, living clarity. The difficulty as the Head of the Department admits, when confronted by his Teacher's problem . . .

. . . 'there is knowing and knowing. Knowing and not knowing. I chose to unknow the source . . .'

No race in the whole world puts more heart and will into the basic celebrations of life. Birth. Marriage. Death. Dates engraved on the hearts of the working class Scot. Yet, somehow, some . . . inexplicable how, never come up to their long anticipated anticipations, as revealed by the younger sister of The Bride at just such a Celebration.

'. . . The Cathedral Service with Nuptial Mass. The big Reception held in the best hotel in the Town. Every relative we possessed who hadn't spoken to any of us for years and would not speak to us again after today. It was a farce. The whole bloody business. A Cock Up . . .'

Nuff said. I leave the reader of Rosemary's story *The Wedding* to discover and enjoy just how *much* of a farce it turned out to be.

In *Exile From Hirta,* Wilma Murray takes as her theme an "old unhappy . . . incident from Scottish history, but still in racial memory; when Crofters in the Highlands were burned out of their homes and deprived of their livelihoods by the order of absentee Landlords to make way for the more profitable venture of sheep breeding.

The strength and beauty of Wilma Murray's evocation movingly captures the effect of total Uprootedness of one such Exile.

. . . 'Her mind, tuned to one song will never learn another. She will wake every morning in a confusion of new geometry, with her old home firmly rooted in her eyes . . .'

She, too, has chosen childbirth as one of her themes. *Don't* be misled by the title of her story, *Old Wives' Tales.* This young mother to be - and you can almost "see" her pacing the floor - confides to the child her apprehensions of the *modern* world her child is about to enter.

'. . . Stay where you are for a while. Have a last swim around in the warm dark.

No star in the East or three wise men for you Kiddo. The world out here's not a place to rush into . . . There's AIDS, drugs and God knows what's all . . .'

Indeed! No Auld Wife would have had a "Remedy" for the apprehensions.

In her story *Widow's Walk* Wilma Murray's Widow has taken the hardest, yet in its way the most effective way of alleviating the pain of bereavement, by confronting it full face on. Allowing it the full gamut of its agony. . . .

'She plucked an old ganzie from his chair by the fire and put it on over her clothes. It smells of him of boats and the sea . . . comforting, warm, familiar . . .'

Taking the road to the busy quayside where every facet of her dead husband's life stabs at her memory, grief itself quietens, stills and - accepts - under such an onslaught . . . A strong story. Beautifully told.

These are but a sample of the short stories in *Three's Company* by young writers and a young brand new Publisher.

JESSIE KESSON

# CONTENTS

# THE CONVEYOR BELT

Sadie Dempster looked, and felt, like a camel which had inadvertently swallowed its hump, as her father handed her over to the granite reception block of the city's maternity hospital. She was his only girl, bearing his first grandchild. He had driven her there, as if conveying a priceless Ming vase in his car. Her husband, John was at work. Her husband, John, disliked hospitals in general and under-par-people in particular. 'Once upon a time', as they said in the best-child-books, it had been a pleasure to be ill, she thought, distributing her double weight uncomfortably on the bench beside another five hatching pregnancies. When she'd been a child, things had been so different . . . her own small room, pleasantly warm, everyone extra-specially nice and caring, and Old Dr Jacob, with his soothing, reassuring manner, who always wore a carnation in his buttonhole, was white-haired (the little that was left of it) as Santa Claus, and just as bountiful, and always preceded every examination by popping a dolly mixture into her mouth. The 5-star treatment.

'And how's my favourite patient today?' he would ask, as if listening to Sadie's wheezes was the zenith of rapture. And when he left, wreaths of Friar's Balsam would be drowsy in the air, the croup-fever spots would be fading into healthy pink on her cheeks, and father would sing to her. That was the best medicine of all, of course. Father had a fine, mellow voice that quite made Sadie forget to cough. 'Go to sleep, my baby, close your pretty eyes,/ Little one, you've had a busy day . . .' For years, Sadie had thought he had composed that very song with her in mind. It had come as a slight shock to realise that it was a common, show-biz ditty.

'Mrs Dempster?' The receptionist shattered the daydream, like breaking a toy. 'Age?' 28. 'Married?' Yes. 'Previous pregnancies?' Nil. 'The first time then?' Yes . . . A nurse relieved Sadie of her case, her clothes and her security, took her temperature, allocated her a bed, opposite a clock. Sadie stared at it, blankly. Such a relief it had been, to stop teaching! It made all the nausea, backache and tiredness of pregnancy worthwhile. To waken each day, to observe that day, white, and wholesome as an egg, that no class could Humpty-Dumpty . . . The day your very own, no pressure, no responsibility, just one long drink of solitary ambrosia . . .

Not that she hadn't made preparations. Of course she had. She'd read all the requisite child-care books, waded through reams of child psychology notes. . . Sadie had no practical experience of infant homo sapiens, but the plastic doll at the classes hadn't complained.

'Remember the six P's,' John told her. 'Prior planning prevents piss-poor performance.' John was an ex-paratrooper. John-Junior would reveille at 6am, feeding to attention, would have been dinnered, snoozed, bathed and taken the air in his pram by 5pm, before his father came home at six. Whereupon, as a good child should, he would sleep till next reveille . . . a mini Action Man. After all, he would have nothing to cry about. He was a planned baby. . .

Sadie's child-rearing ideas differed from John's, vastly. Sadie-Junior would be exposed to a multitude of visual aids. She hoped her son wouldn't be tiresomely scientific. Half of his genes would be hers, for God's sake. He couldn't . . . the thought was intolerable. . . he couldn't be a *total* clone of John. No, Sadie's child was going to be creative, sensitive, artistically and musically gifted. Please God, thank

1

you God, three bags full God. Good looks and a strapping physique were optional extras. Toulouse Lautrec had been no fashion plate; it was creativity that mattered. . .

Within an hour of clocking-in, Mrs Dempster had been rinsed, scrubbed, scoured, shaved, tranquilised, and produced a faeces to order. She was then trolleyed back to her bed, prior to being 'started off' in the morning. The phrase 'starting off' was new to Sadie, it made her sound like a consumptive car, with attached jump leads. It turned out to be the 'in-hospital' jargon for 'artificially induced childbirth'. . . the countdown for take-off. She had just assimilated this information, while sucking yet another thermometer, when a drugs-on-wheels container rattled merrily into view, pushed by a short, puffing handmaiden of mercy. 'Anything for aches, pains, moans or groans, dearie?' she asked, as if dispensing sweets at a large, comprehensive-school playtime. Sadie settled for one white one and two yellow ones, washed down with the hospital's very own sterilised water. Whereupon she was immediately transported by four immaculate storks to a pillow-down-nursery of sleep. . .

Morning was extremely public, a dawn chorus of emptying bedpans, screeching hoovers and hideous apparitions. Sadie's eyes slowly focussed on what appeared, at first, to be a Samurai warrior in angel's garb. . . No, it was a drill sergeant in a self-raising flour factory. . . No, it was the Ward Sister.

'Dear, dear, Mrs Dempster. Whatever did you DO in there last night!' she said reproachfully. An orderly tittered. Sadie was directed to a seat while the offending bed was tidied. Sadie liked an untidy bed. It was one of the greatest tactile pleasures of life, cool linen on warm skin . . . exploring its nooks and crannies, entwining and curling yourself round the pillow, like a somersaulting dolphin sliding over the waves. The Samurai warrior made it sound almost obscene, to enjoy such simple pleasures. Evidently she liked her beds ruler straight. A ward of mortuary stiffs. Angle of Mercy . . . Angel of Nemesis . . . now, for Sadie, just a green shrunken overall (a little accident at the laundry dear) that hung on the camel's hump like a tablecloth draped on a flatulent whale, and a chilly trolley ride, in convoy, to the 'starting-off room'.

When Sadie's turn came to go in, she was amazed to see a hospital disc jockey scrubbing his hands in the sink. He certainly wasn't a doctor. He had a lurid tie and an inane stream of trendy patter, long hair, and blearie eyes. He didn't look a day older than nineteen. He didn't look at Sadie at all, concerned only with the Australian part of her anatomy to the south of where the kangaroo keeps its hanky. 'I'm not down there. I'm up here,' she wanted to protest.

'Climb on the table please. I'm going to break your water,' he said to her uterus. Sadie closed her eyes, clenched her teeth, anticipating excruciating pain, a loud bang and several feet of water to spurt forth like a tapped oil well, all over the disc jockey's tie. She was so intent on listening for the bang, she missed the sight of him wiring her up to a labyrinth of tubes, wires and mysterious machinery. There were tubes running from her arms and wires from unthinkable places; it was like occupying the electric chair at Alcatraz. The machine was ticking like a bomb.

'Baby Dempster's heartbeat, dear.' Dear God, was he going to blow up?

'Mrs Dempster's coming along nicely,' said the nurse to yet another disc jockey

2

- or was he a steward from Air India? It was so confusing, all those strange faces and strange uniforms. 'Coming along nicely!' roared the nurse in Sadie's ear. Sadie wasn't deaf. Was she a roasting chicken, then? If so, she was being done to a slow turn. John-Junior launched into take-off, a roadman's mallet grinding into flesh. At the pre-natal classes the lecturer had made it sound so easy, so chicken licken easy, like a brisk jog. 'Breathe deeply and think pleasant thoughts.' Some jog. Some chicken. The hands of the clock crawled round to twelve. The chicken was falling off the bone in one long rend of sundering, cracking shell. An inhuman howl tore from Sadie's throat, invaded the length of the ward, bringing the Samurai down on her like the wrath of God on a stormy Sunday. 'Now, now, now, Mrs Dempster! That's enough of that. It's only just started.' She propelled Sadie adroitly into a side room, machine attached, and left the cooked chicken simmering. Sadie continued to scream, notwithstanding. Think pleasant thoughts. Right, right. Sister was a huge white jellyfish. A steam roller was pressing Sister into a ten-inch-deep bed of nails. Think Pleasant Thoughts. Sister was a fat flour sack before a firing squad. Rat-at-at-aaaaaoooow. The pain was back again. Bugger, bugger it, bugger it. . .

People flitted in and out, masked and muttering and menacing. Sadie was elastic at the limit of its tension, mind or body would snap at any minute. A second injection of pethedine was administered and then, the bliss of splitting in two of consciousness. Far below her, a hideous, misshapen creature was writhing on a white table. Sadie had severed all connection with the thing on the table, was a high, soft, disembodied mind. But the bubble of safety was dissolving, she was being pulled back down into the pain. The surgeon slit skin.

'Push,' said a voice from behind a mask. And the thing on the table responded, with an extra thrust of sheer terror. Reluctantly, her mind sank back into her body and Sadie Dempster was one again, too numb to feel anything. Completely and utterly exhausted. The camel's hump was ugly folds of slack skin. The real thing had arrived.

It had two arms, two legs, was red, wrinkled and crying, and it was a boy. At least she had managed to get that right. A masked, muffled, anonymous face whispered something about 'pair-bonding', but it was too early for that yet. Mrs Dempster had dropped into a deep pit of sleep.

When Sadie came round, she was in a long, dark ward. A nurse brought her a drink of milk and a wheelchair with a rubber ring on it. For some inane reason Sadie thought the hospital had arranged for her to go sea bathing.

'It says on your notes,' said the nurse a little disapprovingly, 'that you want to feed baby yourself.' Evidently, breast-fed babies curdled-up hospital procedure, the current policy being 'bottle is best'. A crate of sterilised milk lay accusingly in a corner, jam-packed with vitamins and healthful, zestful additives. Sadie inched herself onto the rubber ring, realising that 'the real thing' wasn't occupying a cot beside her bed like all the others.

'He's under the lights, Mrs Dempster. Nothing to worry about. A touch of birth jaundice.'

Under the lights there was a whole platoon of oriental-looking sunbathers, all with green nets over their hair and cotton wool where their eyes should be. My God, her son was blind! He would never hold a paintbrush, visual aids were a non-event.

3

Furthermore, he looked like a frog. Furthermore, there was a tap attached to his navel. . .

'The cotton wool's just to protect his eyes from the rays,' said the nurse. 'And the "tap" will fall off, I do assure you.'

She placed John-Junior into Sadie's arms. His tiny neck twisted like a corkscrew, frantically seeking food. His bird-mouth clamped uselessly on Sadie's arm and sucked stale armpit. The disappointment was too much. He gave up and fell asleep.

'Now, now, Baby Dempster, none of that,' said the nurse. She nipped his heel, quite hard. He gave a surprised yowl and again suckled on arm. The nurse prized his head back and pressed the small jaws, which dropped open like a lid. She shoved his nose firmly into his mother's breast. Nothing happened. He seemed in imminent danger of suffocation. Mother and son went into a downward spiral of disenchanted frustration.

'What's wrong with him? Why won't he feed? Doesn't he *like* me?' wailed Sadie. It was all turning into a nightmare. Inadequate mother = inadequate son. 'Piss-poor performance', as John would say.

'Sometimes,' said the nurse, looking hard at Sadie, 'they take a wee while to get the hang of things.'

The poor child had been yanked from his sunbathing to be starved, nipped, manipulated, and for what? For a mouthful of armpit. Then Sadie noticed the band on his arm. Good grief, this wasn't Auschwitz! Had they tattooed his bum too?

'Mrs Dempster,' sighed the nurse, rapidly losing patience, 'ALL the babies are wearing armbands. Otherwise, however could we tell them apart!'

Sadie surveyed the nursery. It was true. Each child was hairnetted, navel-tapped and armbanded. There was a strong pervasive smell of milk everywhere. For a horrible second it seemed to Sadie that John-Junior was only a small calf, in a very large dairy. She crawled back to bed, swallowed two white pills from the aches and pains trolley and slept till morning, whereupon the Samurai warrior was at her again.

'There is a special hospital procedure for topping and tailing baby.'

Was he a carrot then? Sadie wondered, but sat on the thought, the only thing she *could* sit on that didn't throb. Sister flapped up the wings of a demonstration baby-box with the expertise of a gunner assembling a machine gun.

'Now, we shall have the naming of parts,' muttered Sadie.

'Did you speak, Mrs Dempster?' asked the Samurai-who-looked-like-a-flour-sack.

'I said, it's very hard at the start,' lied Sadie feebly.

'Perhaps you would give us a demonstration . . . with Baby Dempster, of course.'

Baby Dempster, having had a frazzle of a night with his new mother, was extremely grumpy and loath to be demonstrated. He had just spent 20 minutes trying to locate Sadie's left breast, which was now solid with milk and probably turning to Gouda, thought Sadie. He had triumphantly found the left breast when nurse dragged him off and obliged him to hunt for the right breast. Now you have it, now you don't. 'Hospital rules, dearie. 10 minutes each side. Can't have you going home lopsided.' Sister arranged a row of cotton wool, talcum powder, zinc ointment, nappy, muslin liner, soap, water, evil-smelling purple fluid for the tap on the navel, with the rigid attention to detail of Florence Nightingale going off to minister to the dying hordes at Scutari. More medicament than baby.

Sadie's stitches had tightened through the night. A Dr Fissure had inserted them. She was sure he had miscounted and put in some extra. Probably while chatting to the disc jockey or the Air India steward. John-Junior couldn't, or wouldn't, bend, refused to have his arms removed from his clothes. He kicked over the talcum and Sadie dropped him in the basin. He howled indignantly. A whole new baby-box was set up. Sadie applied the tap fluid to his bum and the talcum to his head. After two re-runs, she had just manipulated him onto the nappy when he peed in a rainbow arc all over her. Had he been the plastic doll, she would have melted him down to buttons that very instant.

'Sit DOWN, Mrs Dempster,' said Sister. 'I suppose you know this is ALL FOR YOUR OWN GOOD. I won't be at home to help you.'

'Thank F . . .' thought Sadie in a most un-maternal humour. She made a mental note never to bathe Baby Dempster till her mother came visiting. He would get a quick wipe, a sponge round his posterior and like it, on all other occasions.

After the baby-box was trailed away, thirty mothers lay down on the floor to be exercised.

'Not joining in, Mrs Dempster?' asked the physiotherapist. 'You'll be sorry later. Your uterus might fall down.'

With luck, so might your maternity hospital, thought Sadie. She crept into bed and attempted to find privacy in sleep. Sister prodded her awake. She began to weep silently.

'Baby blues,' said Sister smugly, whipping up the sleeve of Sadie's nightie for the routine blood pressure test. Sadie pretended to be a Dalek incinerating Sister with her eyes. Baby Dempster began to wail. Sadie reached over to lift him up.

'Tut tut tut, Mrs Dempster! We never hold baby in bed. Anyway, too much handling's bad for him.'

How the hell did Sister know? Had she asked John-Junior? Did they *do* a survey of the newly born? Probably, probably, nobody ever handled Sister at all. She wondered if Sister was married and, if so, was copulation routine and disinfected afterwards.

'Intercourse will take place at 11pm exactly,' she could hear Sister say. 'It will last for 10 minutes each side, after which there will be the naming of parts.' The bell for visiting time disrupted the diverting supposings on the nocturnal doings of the Samurai.

Sadie sat up with difficulty, as if impaled on a hedgehog. A posse of Dempsters coagulated in tiny clots around the moody personage in the cot. His jaw was jutting out like Mussolini's.

'Definitely a Dempster nose,' said one. Sadie bristled. He was nothing like the Dempsters. He was the image of her father and, judging by his temper to date, he was going to be highly artistic. The visitors handed Sadie a clump of chrysanthemums and a box of grapes. The bedside began to resemble Interflora. Storks abounded everywhere and little blue boots with ribbons. At home, Baby Dempster's storks were going to be chucked out, replaced by Leonardo cartoons. They then proceeded to forget Sadie, and Baby Dempster too, and chat amongst themselves

5

except for an elderly maiden Dempster who ghoulishly wanted all the blood-curdling details down to the last stitch. John arrived late, in his working clothes, still suffused with celebratory drink. Mercifully, Sister was off duty. He leered at the nurses, patted John-Junior on the head till all one ounce of Sadie's very own milk was erupted by the distressed infant over his pillow, and then demanded to know when Sadie was coming home to resume her wifely duties and attend to HIM. For once, Sadie was glad of the Samurai's strict rules. Visiting time was FAR TOO LONG.

As the Dempsters left, Sadie's father came in. He had taken particular care to dress, and said practically nothing at all, but he looked at John-junior, and beamed. Ten days later, he collected daughter and grandson himself, having persuaded John to allow their first night out-in-the-world to be under his roof. After all, it would take John at least 24 hours to clear away the debris of enforced bachelorhood at the marital home. You couldn't have the district nurse wading through mountains of beercans, and greasy plates.

The real thing, when released from the hot house of the hospital, complained raucously and at length. He cried when Sadie lifted him. He cried when she didn't. He cried when she fed him. He cried when she didn't. People maintained that food was the fount of life. People were wrong. It was sleep, the most blessed, most healing balm of all. Complete, merciful oblivion. John-Senior would have been furious. ''Piss-poor performance all round.'' By midnight, the real thing had howled himself hysterical, and his mother was considering calling the Samaritans. Her father, hearing the rucus, rose and came into Sadie's room. He removed his grandson firmly from the mother, and placed him in his cot. He tucked Sadie up in bed. He returned to the cot, and carried John junior over to a chair. Sitting down with him, he started to rock backwards and forwards. He began to sing, as he has sung to Sadie so many years ago, when she was ill and small and troubled. Now, the wheel had turned full circle. It was his grandson that he sang to. And there was much sweetness and much love in his singing. Warm, secure and wanted, gently slipping off the conveyor belt at last, mother and son closed their eyes and slept.

Sheena Blackhall

6

# TONGS RULE. O.K.

James Anderson set his paint brush down carefully across the rim of the tin, which was rapidly congealing with shiny gloss paint, and sat down to admire his handiwork, wet and glistening on the gate. This legacy of his aunts could not have come at a better time; another year of teaching would have been intolerable. The windy annexe where he worked was a daily tussle with poverty and ignorance. The classroom violence left him physically drained. This house of his aunts was his ticket out of all that.

He stretched his arms contentedly, and made a final inspection of the garden.

It had been in a very disordered state when his aunt had died; years of neglect had made a wilderness of the hedge, now trimmed into regimental order, like a drill sergeant's moustache. The nettles and dandelions choking the parterres had been cleared to make way for small shrubs, each one neat as an entry on a legal register; the lawn was smoother than a drink of milk. He was anxious to impress his new neighbours, comfortable stockbroker types who knew nothing of the sordid fabric of his own line of work. Tomorrow was the first day of his retirement. A clean sheet. He would crumple up the memory of Westway school and toss it into the gutter, ignore the alarm clock for ever after, because tomorrow, time would be all his own to use or misuse as he wanted.

He pitied his replacement. Westway school reeked of stale milk, chalk, and urine. It was a post-war, jerry-built, prefabricated monster, which had slipped through the fingers of a disorganised planning committee and found its way brick by hideous brick on top of a hill ringed by tenements, a stone calvary.

The narrow alleys that trickled like open sewers from its peeling sides led off into half-built roads, foetid with mud, scavenged by packs of dogs, who roamed the estate in fleabitten bravado, as if aware that there was safety in numbers, the discarded pets of the people who brawled, bred, and died in the tenements, where the flats stretched endlessly upwards, a blot on the sky. Graffiti screamed down old warnings, old hatreds in a no-mans land of no-hopers, a human dustbin.

The school itself was circled by high fencing, giving it the air of a prison camp; but the fence was no deterrent to dedicated vandalism. The city fathers tired of funding new glass for broken windows; it was a never ending game, smash and crash, crash and pay up. James had grown accustomed to teaching with windows boarded up in damp card, had become hardened to finding desks ransacked and weeks of work destroyed on a gang spree of ten mindless minutes. After all, his salary was adjusted accordingly, cynically referred to as 'Danger Money'.

If even one child had been worth the effort, in all those years. . . But never, not once, had there been such a being. They were dirty, lice infested, sub-human, rows · of cunning eyes, that he could never reach, the bored sperm of unemployment the illigitimate product of neglect and despair. Social workers made frequent sorties into the estate, as did the police, but their influence was negligible.

To James Anderson, the 50 yard walk to the bus stop and the chilling wait for a bus which was invariably late, was the worst part of the day. Out of school bounds, his flimsy authority, backed by the black Lochgelly tawse in his desk, was meaningless. Then, the ghetto land with its gutter savagery was a living threat. Eyes

7

followed him, returned his timidity with contempt, as if stripping off his tweed accessories, the vestiges of a professional man, and seeing only his weakness and his fear. For he did experience fear on the nightly wait for the bus, of a real and terrible kind, that the ghetto would claim him, body and soul, that one day, he would not be able to step on a bus, and leave it behind. . .

Recently, his job had grown worse. There was a new boy in his class, a lad of about 12, who had set out from the start to defy him. He was a big, vicious boy; James's uneasy discipline was shattered. A fornight into the term, James had appealed to the headmaster to have the newcomer, Cassidy, expelled. The head was brusque, and unsympathetic. The problem must be contained. James must use perseverence, dedication. That was, after all, what he was paid for.

It was easy for the headmaster to talk, James thought bitterly. The headship was an administrative post. He spent his time working out time tables and composing high-flown circulars to send to parents incapable of understanding them. He was new, young, and idealistic. And he did not have to face Cassidy each morning, did not have to watch that hard little face twist into a sneer of defiance.

Yesterday, Cassidy had gone too far. He had called James over on the pretext of seeking help with a written question, and had deliberately, with cocky emphasis, spat on his hand. To James, who was meticulously clean in his habits, it was too vile to be tolerated. He slapped the boy's face.

"Hit me, wid ye, ye fuckin' shit" Cassidy shouted.

"That's mair nur yer job's worth, ye bastard."

The class tensed, like a wakened animal. Back off now, and they'd all be onto him. The Lochgelly cracked across the desk.

"Out Cassidy. Now." It was all James would trust himself to say.

To his surprise, Cassidy complied. He swaggered out with maddening insolence, raising his hand to meet the slap of the tawse with ill-feigned amusement. He was playing with the teacher, making a fool of him.

"Gie's it then, ye cunt. I'm nae bothered."

Six times, James brought the belt down, with all the force his arm could muster. The smile slid from a smirk into a twist of pain, the wee hard man melted into exactly what it was, a brutalised, vengeful bairn.

"See you, Mr Anderson," he said, when the teacher had returned the Lochgelly to his desk.

"You watch yersel. Wan o' thay nights, I'm gonna cut ye. . ."

But all that was behind him now. Westway school, Cassidy, were light years off from this pleasant house with the quiet garden. Tomorrow, his last day of teaching. . .

He pressed the lid hard on the paint pot and took it down to the shed. Outside, he could hear the sound of laughter drifting up from the small licensed hotel at the corner. A celebration of some kind seemed in order; nothing too extravagant, for James Anderson was a naturally abstemious man. He lit up a pipe and went back to the house, for a last critical look before turning the key in the door. A little haven; here, he could moor himself quietly into old age. Westway school might exist in Outer Mongolia, he would take care that his former job would not soil this place; he would cut the memory out, like a cancer. He rubbed his hands gleefully.

8

The hotel was almost deserted when he arrived. Synthetic music blurred from a loudspeaker above the bar; two couples sat in subdued chatter, in civilised isolation. A splendidly discreet district, a place where people minded their own business, didn't get involved with unpleasantness. Financially and socially secure. Just the ticket for a retired teacher. He tapped out his pipe, and finished a small sherry. It was a lovely night, he had the Avenue to himself. Firelight glowed from behind each curtained house, a soothing glow, that warmed him.

His gate, recently painted, was round the next corner. He quickened his steps, then stopped, in incredulous disbelief. Dripping along the grain of the gate, like a gashed mouth, like a whore's lipsticked smear, were the words 'Tongs Rule. O.K.'. There was a rustling noise, and Cassidy stepped from the thin protection of the hedgerow. With a dry, wobbly feeling, James Anderson heard the click of a knife. "I've bin waitin for youse, Mr Anderson, ever sic a lang time . . . a wee hoose warmin present". . .

Sheena Blackhall

# THE ROUP

Chay Dalroy hung the last strap of harness carefully on a hook in the barn, before stepping out to face the bare fields. Hard by, to the west, was Leezie's wood, a mass of birk, rowan, and tangled dead bramble briers that ringed his farm like a shield - his farm, and his father's before him, lying silent under the morning mist that curled away in snakes tails before him.

It was early spring in the howe, and the snow clung stubbornly to the hills. The land lay bare, almost begging you to plough it, dour, coorse land that wore you down, year in, year out. But not any more - not after today. Calving ropes, hoes, forks, coils of binder twine and dark rows of machinery were set out, unfamiliarly inactive, waiting for the roup to begin.

There had been a time when Dundore had been a fine farm to fee, before the young laird had come, with his college talk of modernisation that you would need a degree to understand - aye, and even then it would have been hard to make the leap from the safe, known ways. Chay Dalroy understood well enough though, when the rent was raised. It had been the final straw.

His wife Molly was town bred and cared nothing for the place. They went together to dances and to marts, her laugh a little too bright, his drinking a shade too heavy, no better or worse than most. Like a bad hairst, they made the best of things. He had watched her pert prettiness turn to shrewish middle age, had grown weary of her nagging. The shallow gaiety that had once inflamed me, had long since burned out its attractiveness. Maybe now, with the prospect of a town house to retire to, she would give him peace.

Their son John would be pleased. It had never occurred to Chay that John would be anything other than a farmer. He had taken him from a bairn, wrapped in an old rug at the foot of the tractor, teaching him every stick and stone of Dundore as his father had done with him. But there would be no more Dalroys in the place, not now, not ever. John had left in the autumn to begin an apprenticeship as a mechanic in a garage in town. That was what Chay Dalroy got, for marrying a town bred woman folk said, and it had broken his heart.

There was an hour in hand before the roup was due to begin. Chay found himself wandering towards the wood, for he could not settle. His father had taken him there to eat their lunch at hairst times, where it was shady and cool. He remembered a conversation they had had, sitting together in a pool of sunlight, midgies dancing around them, like blown chaff.

"I wish we owned Dundore, da," Chay had remarked, "Instead o' just rentin' it."
"Happen we dinna own it, laddie," came the reply. "But whyles, I think that mebbe it owns us."

Chay had thought that a gey queer thing to say - but now, when it was too late, he half knew what the old man had meant. He thought of what his retirement would be - a small house in suburbia, filled with trash from the catalogues that his Molly so admired, with a postage stamp of a garden. He had kept a pig with a larger pen to move around in.

Just as he turned to leave the wood, he could hear a child's laugh - high and brittle. He paused, and stopped in his tracks. What bairn was here, at this hour? They should all be at school. . . He brushed aside a branch, and caught sight of the truant - a boy, dressed in breeches that went out of fashion over half a century ago. And then, Chay's heart turned over, for the boy had his own father's eyes, and his father's queer, lop-sided smile - and that was a thing unthinkable. Before his gaze, the child seemed to melt away. A trick of the light - that would be it. He was not an imaginative man. Maybe he was grown as old and useless as his Molly always said he was. But the sun had fled, and the wind was wintry. . .

He walked slowly home to the empty house. Molly was far way, already settling into their new home. As he entered the kitchen, a flypaper flapped idly at the window. Stacks of plates lay waiting the auctioneer's hammer, tidy and ticketed, like the things in the field - a lifetime's possessions, pegged out for the highest bidder. He sighed, and rummaged in a drawer for the comfort of his pipe and tobacco stopping to pick up his father's pistol - a relic of the First World War. It should fetch a good price today. Beside it was his father's diary. With half an hour in hand before the roup began, he sat down to flick through the pages. The last entries were scrawled, written after the old man had taken to bed in his final illness, but still clear enough to read.

''Thanks be to God, the hairst is in. He is a fine boy, Chay. I can rest easy now, for it would have greived me sore to see Dundore in a stranger's hands; it is my greatest comfort to know that he will carry on. Thy will be done.''

There were no further entries. Chay Dalroy closed the book slowly; at last, at last, the full implication of the roup was sinking in. He thought of the bairn in Leezie's wood, and of himself in his new house in town, lost in the middle of a great city, a useless spent old man, like a bull that has outlived its purpose.

The auctioneer who came to Dundore that day was brisk and methodical. If Chay Dalroy wasn't thère to greet him, so be it. He would start without him. It took some farmers like that, at the last.

Buyers jostled round, keen eyed, on the lookout for bargains, indicating by a dry nod, wink, or tug of the bonnet, that they wanted to buy. Dalroy had aye kept a trim byre; soon, his bits and pieces were carted off across the hills, in rickety trucks and carts. Boxfuls of tools clanked up to the auctioneer's table and were hammered down in quick sale. They were cannie folk in the howe. Nothing of value would be missed.

But with the bulk of the machinery and stock gone, people drifted away. Only domestic items remained to be sold, though the antique dealers were anxious to see them. There were brose bowls and giant ashets that had not seen service since the days of the shire horses - the Americans would like those. The remaining bidders, chattering and joking, turned towards the house.

The auctioneer entered the kitchen, keeping up a cheery dialogue, and then froze, for once, lost for words. For resting on the table, amidst dishes and cutlery, a smile fixed on his lips, and an old leather diary in his left hand, was the master of Dundore. He could almost have been asleep, but for the small red hole at his temple, and the slim trickle of blood that ran like a scratch to his cheek. Chay Dalroy would not be leaving, after all. . .

Sheena Blackhall

11

# THE SWINGING SIXTIES

Alastair gazed into Morag's eyes. The sun was slipping down beside the loch. He was looking at her as if he's just seen her for the first time. Love had come to Kirkintilloch.

'Annie!' Mrs Reid shook her daughter's shoulder impatiently. 'Annie, will ye pit doon that rubbishy magazine, an' rin roon tae the bakers fur a loaf.' Annie set down the passionate saga of Alastair and Morag with reluctance. *True Romance* was much more interesting than the collection of a packet of yeasty stodge. She took the money sulkily, and mooned over to the mirror to pluck out some offending eyebrows. Her eyebrows ran together like a thatch. It was most unfair - between that and a preponderance of plooks, nature seemed determined to blight her growing vanity.

Her mother groaned. Last year Annie had been happy to stot her ball against the garage door, cheery in ankle socks. Now it was constant back-chat and a mini-skirt verging on the indecent. Besides, Annie's thighs were far too fat to be improved by exposure; her back-combed hair made her look like a frightened hedgehog. Her mother took down a scrubbing brush and pummelled the mascara stains on the virginal-white pillowcase. That was another thing - it was inevitable that the girl would discover cosmetics - but did she have to clart them on with a trowel? Now she was wanting to go to the local dance - her wee Annie, that hated the sight of boys.

Mrs Reid recalled her own first dance; her father's words rang ominously back over the years, doleful through the soap suds: 'And mind an' be in by ten o'clock., I'll nae hae a dother o' mine ca'd a whoor.' Aye, the same rules held good today, she thought. The lads had all the fun. The Swinging Sixties were grand for a few painted trollops down in London, but in the village, Calvin still reigned supreme. An actress in Soho could drop as many 'love children' as she liked - in Annie's village they kenned a bastard when they saw one.

The bakery was practically deserted, but the handful of customers were enjoying their shopping. Annie scuffed her heels wearily over the door. She's been to Aberdeen once, and had been amazed at the speedy service there. The assistants had raced through the queues like a dose of salts. Nobody asked how you were in the city, or bored you rigid with the minutiae of last night's rural meeting. Nobody noticed if your buttons were squint, or made you stand till your feet went numb, while they discoursed with the person in front as to the incontrovertible fact that Dr Masters smelt of drink when he lanced Mrs Paterson's boil.

In short, the town was so chic, so high-powered, life in the fast lane, where the action was.

'Onythin' new wi' you, Annie?' asked the shopgirl, flicking open a paper bag with skilled precision. Ballooning with pleasure, Annie stepped forward. Her turn for the limelight. She lingered over the announcement, teasing out the small triumph.

'Could be, could be. As a matter of fact . . .' she paused to prod a marshmallow, 'I'm goin' tae the dance the nicht.'

The shopgirl smirked, rather unpleasantly Annie thought.

'Watch oot for the guard, Annie. They're a gey faist lot.'

Annie rather hoped they might be . . . it added spice to the anticipation.

'The guard' was a blanket term used in the village for the lorryloads of uniformed youths who descended on the tiny hamlet when the Royal Family came north for their summer vacation. Her Majesty always had a Scots regiment billeted near at hand on these occasions, though it was not a favourite posting with the men.

The barracks were too small to accommodate married quarters, and if the scenery was spectacular, the entertainment (for the red-blooded military male) was nil. Most had seen service in Aden, Cyprus and Germany . . . but there were no exotic strip clubs in Annie's village, just a fish and chip shop and the Saturday night dance. No oriental lovelies to wink them on through henna'd curls - just rows of fishnet stockings, amply filling chairs around the hall like a trawling fleet in full sail, out to trap a sprat.

Surprisingly, given the circumstances, love did occasionally blossom, or rather, lust gone wrong. Every year at least one local girl would lead a pimply, gangling Lowlander to the altar, stiffly bodiced into her off-white wedding dress, deserting the hills of her fathers for squalid little married quarters. There, to be lost in a labyrinth of faceless, cosmopolitan neighbours, who by promiscuity and drunkenness, whiled away their grass widowhood.

Other local girls were less fortunate. They saw in these glib, experienced soldiers the chance to break out of the village, before the hills closed in and swallowed them whole - they threw themselves recklessly at every man in tartan trews or a kilt. Betty McPhee was one such - twenty-four years old, with four bairns to bring up: a Cameronian, an Argyll and Sutherland Highlander, a Gordon and a Black Watch. Village gossip had it that even the Boys' Brigade would not be safe - the lassie having such a weakness for uniforms. Annie had been aware of the guard for some time. Giggling convoys of her girlfriends wandered aimlessly back and forth outside the barracks flirting with the sentry who stood sweatily to attention in full kit, or else they peered wistfully through the fence at so much pent-up manly charm, like penniless bairns ogling a tray of sweeties.

On Saturdays, the regimental band gave a display of piping on the village green. They marched out from their quarters, the pipe-major flinging a huge, sparkling mace high before him; pipes skirling, drummer fierce in leopard skin, swanking out in heavy tartan - all spanking clean, with belts and knives bulled to perfection, strong hairy limbs striding out in perfect symmetry. Small boys blew bubblegum and ancient curs scratched at pubic fleas as they passed, but Annie thought the military was wonderful. So noble - each like a real chieftain. You couldn't really blame Betty McPhee.

On Games Day the soldiers competed in the hill race, an arduous event, and to the chagrin of the local boys the soldiers always won, their long trained legs bounding up the tortuous scree to the summit, like mountain hares. Oh yes, Annie was ready for the dance.

It took her an hour to get ready, like a pharaoh being prepared for entombment. Her hair reached unheard of heights of lacquer, her skirt was hitched up so high it resembled a belt. A thin red line of cotton that stood between her and total revelation.

'Be back by midnicht,' her father warned. Safely out of earshot, Annie replied, 'Dis he think I'm Cinderella or somethin'? I'll come hame in my ain time - nae his.'

The hall was like a wedding where nobody's turned up. Jock Sim was at the door, guarding the wee tin takings box and the blue ink stamp that dispensed with the need for tickets - like a shepherd about to brand his flock. He rolled the date stamp over Annie's outstretched hand. Her palm was sweating - the inky numbers blurred. Tomorrow, she thought, it'll aye be there - proof positive I've been here at aa.

Jock looked tired - he'd had only two hours to sweep away the debris of the flower show. Two bookings in one day was too much - they expected miracles on the pittance they paid him as hallkeeper. Here and there, wet petals still clung to the floorboards. He ran his fingers under his white collar and hitched up the breeks of his best suit. Neil Reid's girl coming to the dance. Well, well. It seemed just yesterday he'd been at her christening. Suddenly he felt old. He was surprised that Neil let his girl out, tarted up like that, especially with the guard here - she couldn't be a day older than fifteen. But she'd aye been a wild lassie. He permitted himself a moment of lust, let his eyes linger on the firm, rounded haunch of her. If she dressed like that, she deserved all she got.

Annie circled the hall disconsolately, conspicuous in the isolation. Last time she'd been here, a sale of work had been in progress. Old lampshades and down-at-heel boots. The Blue Varmints were tuning up for the evening's performance . . . the usual selection of eightsome reels, quickstep country and western airs, saving the waltzes till last. By the end, the couples would be paired off, would have arrived at the heave and squeeze stage, engaged in voyages of mutual intimate exploration, like surgeons feeling for bumps. Also, most of the men would be totally inebriated. Now, a drunk can wreak untold havoc in an eightsome reel, but in a waltz situation only slithers harmlessly to the floor, or wilts, doe-eyed, into the bosom of his beloved. The Blue Varmints always played *Danny Boy* at the end - by then the audience was awash with John Begg whisky and sentiment, and it brought it all to a soggy crescendo.

Annie was disappointed. No men had turned up at all, as the shopgirl could have told her . . . none would, either, till the pubs closed. Jock Sim, taking advantage of the lull in admissions, dragged her round the floor in a furious Gay Gordons - a dance not suited to mini-skirts or girls with excessively large thighs. It was a relief when the music jarred to a halt. She ran for the cover of the ladies' lavatory, ostensibly to powder her nose.

The lavatory was a primitive retreat reminiscent of a log cabin, with an antique sink capable of bathing a baby rhinoceros. Suspended above it from a surly nail hung a large cracked mirror, and two Brasso tins lids sat on the window ledge, doubling as ashtrays.

Outside, three girls sat, smoking balefully. One of them was swigging whisky from a gill bottle. Annie stared at her, incredulous.

'Somethin' wrang wi' your face?' inquired the drinker. 'The dance should be licensed. God - ye'd need a drink tae look at the talent hereaboot.'

Annie knew the girl slightly - she came from a neighbouring village and only visited the place when the guard was in residence.

A sudden spasm of music from the Varmints announced that at long last the talent had arrived. The girls tensed, became predatory, affected poses. One or two managed a pout. Some of the lads were quite handsome - a few were Gaelic speakers, the soft seductive sing-song of the west. It wasn't etiquette to ask a boy up that you fancied - you needed brass neck for that. One by one the older girls, more experienced at giving a sly 'come on', were snapped up by partners. It was like sitting through a roup - all around folk were bidding, but somehow Annie couldn't master the signs.

Her mascara was running, and a splinter from the rickety bench had laddered her stockings. She had borrowed her mother's suspender belt, and it was digging into her crotch. Nobody asked her up, nobody at all. By eleven o'clock she was near to tears. The shopgirl was there, reeking of scent, ridiculously old-fashioned in a Vera Lynn frock with peep-toe sandals. Probably her granny's, Annie thought spitefully. Yet even she had found a lad - a gawky, leering farmer, with great raw hands, pawing her round the floor like a butcher manoeuvring a prime joint. He had an accent so thick you could break stones on it, acne, and jug ears, yet he held the shopgirl tight and she seemed to enjoy it. Monday morning was going to be horrendous - everyone would know that only Jock Sim, as macho as wet cabbage leaf, had asked her up.

Ten minutes from the end, Birkie McGregor came in to collect the crates of lemonade. His father supplied the soft drinks for the Saturday dances - he was about Annie's age, a shy, stammering boy, in Fair Isle jersey and grey flannels. The other lads called him a jessie. As he bent to hoist the crates, Annie seized a pinchful of flannel and nipped him hard. Birkie McGregor jumped up in alarm.

'Tak me hame, McGregor, or I'll tell yer dad I saw ye smokin' roon the back o' the chippers.'

Birkie went stickly pale, opening and shutting his mouth like a stranded salmon.

'Bit it's a secret . . .' he stammered.

'A secret? In this place?' Annie was derisive. She began to wheedle. 'It's nae as if I'd asked ye tae mairry me - jist walk me hame . . .'

Gallantly, Birkie obliged. As they reached Annie's door he began to assume the pose of a stalking heron, contorting his neck as if about to give her a quick peck.

'Bugger aff, McGregor - ye mak' me puke,' said the girl. He stumbled off down the road, totally confused.

On Monday, the shopgirl served up the loaf with a smile. *She'd* got a lad all right - she'd the love bites to prove it, strung round her neck like an African's baubles.

'Did ye nae fancy the guard, Annie?' she sneered.

'Oh aye,' said Annie, coolly. 'It wis a' yon Birkie McGregor's fault - pestered me aa nicht. Nae gettin' rid o' him. I didna like tae say no, wi' mam workin' part time in his faither's shop. Ye ken how it is.'

The shopgirl smiled. She rather thought she did.

Sheena Blackhall

15

# RUTH

John Ballantyne and I'd been friends from years back. We'd gone from catapults and marbles together to long trousers and full strength Capstan cigarettes at the same village school. We'd chased Molly Heseltine, the village belle, through the same straggly grass at the edge of the golf course, and sickened on the same ale, with the village darts team, on market days when our fathers were too tipsy to notice the froth around our beardless lips.

Two streams diverging quite naturally, we had branched off from our common ancestral pool of Sunday cricket, vicarage teas, and family picnic outings, John, to college and a teaching post I heard, and myself, from a firm of accountants, to business adviser with a large international oil company. There's nothing either glamorous or risky in accounting, but there WAS a certain charm about being constantly mobile, that being my company's policy towards financial senior executives... lessening the likelihood of corruption, the directors said, keeping the local staff on their toes, by flying in a new man always to check the books...

Well, I enjoyed the travelling, in the main, but just occasionally it palled. Being a hotel nomad grew tiring. I felt the need of a little break, and the notion grew that I'd like to spend it somewhere, or with someone, familiar. I'd formed no definite plans on the matter, when by a happy coincidence, a fortnight before my annual leave was due, who should I meet near our Paris office, but my friend John Ballantyne, struggling out of the metro, like a caterpillar glued into its skin, with a trail of children in tow. He had the same, red freckled face, and red, carroty hair, I recalled as a youth, even the same slightly worried expression as if he'd swallowed a worm by mistake, and wasn't sure which end it'd come out of.

As his class milled around him, he caught sight of me, over their caps and clamour. He ushered them onto a waiting bus, and hurried over to me, for a brief word.

"Good to see you, George," he said, with the terseness of a dot under an exclamation mark. "There's a cafe at Montmartre, The Black Cat . . . it's quiet and not too expensive. Come if you can. Can't stop! About nine . . .?" And he scurried off, leaving me smiling and bemused. Quiet, and not too expensive summed John Ballantyne up precisely. . . The sober virtues. Yes, I'd like to meet him again, it would be interesting, like checking my progress against a yardstick, measuring up the years, plus for plus.

I paid the bill, of course. He protested a little, but feebly. Secretly, on a teacher's wage, he must have been rather relieved. But he made a gesture of repayment; after the fifth cognac, he invited me to spend my fortnight's holiday with himself and his family. Insisted on it, in fact. Wouldn't hear of anything else. After the eighth cognac, I agreed.

He'd married a Durham girl, he told me, and bought a house in an outlying rural village. My heart leapt up, at the thought of walks through the English countryside, and dashed down again, at the thought of the wife, Jenny. Damned unpredictible things, wives. And there were children, too. Three, I believe he'd said, two boys and a girl. . . The upshot was, I went.

It was a splendid July morning, as I stepped off from the train, so splendid and

16

sunny and welcoming, such perfect holiday weather, that the clouds were ice cream cool, and the winds were skittish balloons, tugging in excitement to be off. I dispensed with the services of a taxi, and walked the last two miles to John's house. The grass was refreshingly green, civilised and controlled, close cropped lawns, surrounded by heavy honeysuckle, sweet scented lilac, with quaint houses, red bricked and spruce, standing to attention in front of the sky. The houses had long, flowerful gardens, and well tended vegetable plots, each with a dusting of cabbage white butterflies flapping in the greenery like a gnome's washing.

The village had no unifying plan, but seemed to be like a box of child's bricks, thrown down at random. A street would straddle the road, and lead to a farm, which might lead, in turn, to a post office, which in turn might lead to a pond. It had no centre, as such, but existed in autonomous units. Only the red brick, of which each and every structure appeared to be built, gave it an air of belonging together. I came to a ramshackle farm, with a broken mill wheel slumbering at the foot of a gate, and a horse trough, quite close to the road. Here, the road was so rutted, that traffic must have been a novelty, rather than an annoyance.

I rested a moment, for the sun was exceptionally fierce, and bathed my face in the trough. Behind me, arose a cackling and crackling and clattering, like a handful of chestnuts exploding on an Autumn fire. A denuded, featherless fowl, see-sawed around the dust, its neck, ostrich scraggy, its legs and body shrunk to emaciation, its round, pepper-seed eyes, watery and sharp with fright. Following in fast pursuit, came a flurry of cocks, hens, and small to piddling size chickens pecking viciously at the few remaining plumes on its pitiful rump.

The door of the farmhouse swung open, and a stout, matronly woman rushed out, shooing the poultry away with a tin tray, from their quarry. The moulted chicken scuttled thankfully off on its dry-twig legs, into a clump of dandelions.

Its saviour noticed me, and blushed.

"Runt of the litter," she explained. "Nature's way, I expects. But it's not nice, is it? Not nice at all!"

I gave her a broad grin, and nodded agreement. "A bully's a bad piece of work, feathered or human," I agreed.

Hearing a stranger's voice, her own brood emerged shyly from the house, four or five ruddy-faced kids, all with their mother's round face, and sturdy build.

"No piners there, anyway," I remarked.

"Oh no," she agreed. "I treats them all equal, you see. Me and my Harry don't hold with favourites."

The subject originally under discussion, seeing the coast was clear, nervously left its hiding-hole, and strutted up to the hens' seed tin. It was empty. Mrs Harry (for I hadn't been told her name) snatched it up, and ordered the children into the house, to bring out more seed to replenish it. Then she lifted the bird solicitously, to see how much damage it has suffered. Small trickles of blood oozed from the blue-pecked pimples of flesh, on the wing stumps. I gave a grimace of disgust; the chicken was rank as rotting hay, though not that, either. It was hard to define exactly what the smell was . . . it was a curious mixture of dead weeds, abandoned rosebuds, putrid wounds, and damp mushrooms, picked from a fetid tomb; of rancid, six week old pork, of running sores and craters of pus, of cat-pish, vomit, and slime, of a hundred and ninety nastinesses, brewed together in one ghastly nauseus stench, that made my belly flop within me, and my mouth swallow hard.

"God, it smells ripe, though," I explained.

"I can't smell nothing," she returned. "Hens all smells the same to me. This un's a bit unwanted, that's all. The rest dislikes it. Can't smell dislike, now can ee?"

The children had filled the seed tin, and topped up the hens' dish with water. Setting it down, she watched it sup, greedily, then dart off into the bushes again before the others came after it.

"Won't thrive, though," Mrs Harry remarked. "Others are too set agin it. Peck it and peck it they will, until it runs away, or it's done for."

There was no condemnation in her voice, merely acceptance. I asked her, then, where the schoolmaster, Ballantyne, lived, and found he stayed two fields up.

I expected John to greet me himself. Silly, really, I should have realised it would be his wife. I hadn't prepared myself for that, not straight off. I hadn't thought of Jenny Ballantyne at all, other than being John's other half, if you know what I mean. I'd only a batchelor's acquaintance with marriage, businessmen's wives in the main. They were usually employed, if that's the correct word, by their husbands, to hostess, and sweet-talk, and dinner-party, potential clients. Don't get me wrong . . . a good wife can be a first class asset. Except John wasn't a businessman and his wife wasn't an asset, not by a long way. She blocked the door like a jail warden or a night-club bouncer, vetting me with her eyes. The unspoken hostility was unwarranted and irritating.

"I'm sorry John's not here to meet you," she said, in a tone that suggested she couldn't care less either way. "He's out at a meeting. He's always out at a meeting. A schoolmaster's expected to do that, in a small village. Look after everyone elses' kids, no time for his own!"

"I'm sorry," I said, wishing to God I'd never come.

"Oh that's alright, I'm used to it. Well you'd better come in, though you'll find it lean pickings, after the life YOU'VE led, I bet."

I gave a start at that. Jenny had done her homework on me, alright. But I knew nothing at all about her, and by the sound of things, it was her I'd be spending most of my holiday with. I began mentally considering various excuses to extricate myself from this holiday before it had begun. I could see she resented my intrusion into her home. For it was HER home, there was a curious feminine bias about everything in the place. Everything was in apple-pie order, Sunday-school neat, best-behaviour tidy, sweet, and sickly, and . . . suffocating.

She sat me down in a plush, foam-filled sofa. I sank dutifully into it, exploring the contents of the living room, and its owner, with my eyes, as she set a small, snack salad, meticulously, on a low coffee table, and switched on a radiator, despite my protests of excessive heat. I concluded she would not drive me away by coolness, I was to be broiled into leaving.

My hostess had two of the flattest eyes, I have ever seen, fish-shaped and anchor-grey. She had a long, thin face, colourless as a communion wafer, and lips stretched tight-transparent over prominently large teeth. It gave her the horsey expression, some of our lower species of cartoonist are wont to bestow on the Royal family. Her complexion was grey, and her dress was pink, an odd reversal of colour, I thought as if the clothes were the only alive bit about her. The pleasantest area of her anatomy, was her hair, which hung soft and fine like a pony's, and pale as wheat.

I suppose John fitted into this house somewhere, but for the life of me, I couldn't think where. There wasn't a book, nor an ashtray, as much as a stray jotter, to be seen. Perhaps she kept him in the fridge, where the salad had been, I reflected. It looked limp and lifeless enough to have spent a decade there.

It was almost a relief to hear her children come home from school; two boys and a girl, as John had said. Davie, and Frank, and Ruth, I recalled, pleased to have remembered that much. I wouldn't have said the boys resembled their father at all. A shaft of late afternoon sun slanted between the curtains, framing Jenny Ballantyne with her boys. The trio looked uncannily like three wheat sheaves, pale, and close, and whispering. I caught the words 'Daddy' and 'Daddy's friend'. The boys turned their mother's flat eyes on me, in a friendless appraisal.

Well, I've seen Dutch paintings like that let me tell you . . . perfect, but cold, and somehow heartless. They made a finely balanced composition, mother and sons. They belonged together alright, a matching set.

It was the girl, Ruth, that really caught my attention. Shy little thing, she was, hanging back at the door, with that slightly worried expression John always wore and a thatch of red, carroty hair, that took my heart straight out to her. She'd get some tormenting with a mop like that at school, from the other kids, till she'd grown a bit, and then . . . well she'd make a lovely woman, quite striking, like some ancient warrior princess, a head of hair like that. The worried expression deepened I expected Mrs Ballantyne to draw her into the company, to introduce me, but she'd already forgotten my existence, fussing over her two boys like a brewer's dray. I half believed they might all three whinney and stampede off to the kitchen, tossing their manes of wheat.

The little girl slowly came over the room, going not to her mother, but to me. That was quite a surprise, such a shy child, too. She took out her books and pencils and set them down at my table. The lessons were easier than a girl of Ruth's age should be doing, but though she completed the work slowly, she did it neatly, and well. The worried little face, so like her father's, drooped over the schoolbooks despondently, I thought.

Her mother neither praised nor condemned her efforts, but she took much care with the boys' homework, explaining and encouraging difficult points until they were clearly understood.

"Little Ruth here's drawn a lovely flower," I butted in, unsolicited. I could have bitten off my tongue. The mother turned, and eyed the girl dispassionately, as one would an interesting frog, if one were a French chef.

"Ruth's a pretty child, as you see," she remarked. "It's her one virtue, and a fortunate one, I think you'll agree. A career won't matter for Ruth, even were she clever enough to want one. I expect she'll make some man very happy." I thought it an odd speech for a mother to make; chilling, almost.

When we sat down to a late supper, nothing that Ruth could do would please her mother. If she asked for more, she was greedy. If she toyed with her food, she was thriftless. If she talked, she was forward. If she remained silent, she was sulky. I should never have interfered; I couldn't help it. I thought to endear her to her mother, by a simple compliment. I observed how like Jenny, her daughter was. The mother winced, as if I'd struck her a blow.

"You think so, do you? Well I can't see it, I'm sure. She's her father's double, that one, not a bit of me about her."

I repeat, I should never have interfered. You cannot alter December, a rock slide, an iceberg. Such things are unalterable; they operate under natural law. Like it or not, they run their own course, impervious to outside meddling.

I made my excuses abruptly, and left. Mrs Ballantyne was rightly surprised, of course, and I don't mind saying, I'd a stiff letter from John on the subject that took some answering. But I've been a businessman long enough to know how to write a tactful reply, and I think he believed the cock and bull tale I spun him about 'forgetting an urgent appointment with a very important client'. I sent them a present, too, a hideously expensive crystal decanter, with goblets, that went a long way to smoothing over my departure. I couldn't have told him the real reason I left. I couldn't tell anyone THAT.

It was because of Ruth, you see. The more her mother picked on her, the stronger grew that smell, as rank as rotting hay, though not that, either. It was hard to define exactly what the smell was . . . a curious mixture of dead weeds, abandoned rosebuds, putrid wounds, and damp mushrooms, picked from a fetid tomb; of rancid, six week old pork, of running sores and craters of pus, of cat-pish, vomit, and slime, of a hundred and ninety nastinesses, brewed together in one ghastly, nauseus stench that made my belly flop within me. Silly, really. You can't smell dislike, now can you?

Sheena Blackhall

# LETTING GO

The old woman caught the last few words of the news and pressed the on/off button on the radio. She squeezed a tea bag between the rim of her cup and the back of her spoon, and dropped it into the drainer. It made nothing like as good tea as the leaves, but the filling of the pot seemed a terrible waste. The milk, almost turned by yesterday's humidity, left yellow spots floating on the reddish-brown surface. It was the kind of concoction Wullie would have shaken his head at, but her standards were her own now, slowly yet noticeably lowered as year followed year since his funeral.

She shuffled over to the fireside chair, and holding her cup at arm's length, bent almost double, she carefully lowered herself into it, Wullie's chair. She still called it that because it was the gentleman's version in a pair they had bought at great expense when they were in middle-age. Wullie had said, just the once, "We're a childless couple," so long after her change of life, that the statement brought a shock to her which she had thought she could never feel about it again.

After that, he bought the two chairs, proudly bearing them in, the only furniture that was shop-purchased, including the marriage-bed handed down from her Mother. But the Lady's chair, flimsier altogether, and not nearly so comfortable, forcing her as it did into an upright, unnatural posture, wore badly. She covered the seat of it with a cushion, and conscientiously sewed embroidered squares onto the thread bare arms. Shortly after the funeral she threw it out, having, in case she was accused of waste, half-heartedly offered it to Wullie's sister. Now, she sat in Wullie's chair, deep in the cushions, knowing she could lay her head back and close her stinging eyes at will.

She switched the cup to her left hand and picked up the poker, raking the ashes through till she hit clinker. She would light the fire later, about mid-afternoon, even though she could tell that the day would be hot again, like yesterday. Flies, already half-doped, were droning at the window screens and she had not bothered to roll up her stockings. One side of each leg was criss-crossed with purple from sitting too close to the fire the night before. But she loved the leaping life of the flames, and the satisfaction of having laid the sticks and coal, the twisted newspaper, the blazing taper and the nurtured beginnings.

The fire was about all in the way of housekeeping that she did anymore. She had almost given up cooking. What was there to cook for one that didn't involve huge expense and, in the end, waste. The smallest chicken yielded up its last pleasures for her at the end of three days and the last of it went in the bucket. So she lit a fire instead, every day of the year, and ate her cold dripping sandwiches beside it. One expense at least spared, since the time was past when she fetched her coal off the beach behind her house, one in a row backed by the high sea wall. For years she had joined the other women, tying up the corners of her apron and dropping in the small lumps of coal which had been washed up from long-sunk coal boats.

With practise, she had learned to spot the high quality lumps and could take her place amongst the best of the gatherers. But she could still squirm at the memory of how, newly-arrived with her groom in the village, the gathering women had plied her with pieces of solid tar, to her no different from coal. How they must have laughed at the time and later, when in hopeless panic, minutes before Wullie's return from work, she had watched the scorching lumps melt and drip their irremovable patches onto her polished hearth. They had taught her early on that there was more to inclusion in the ranks than marrying one of their sons.

And the setting apart hadn't been helped as year after year her flat belly had turned mouths behind shawls and called out words of spite from her mother-in-law. Not that anything had been said in front of Wullie. But he had known. Once, at a social, on the edge of a circle of presented backs, he had firmly led her forward, defying the rules, and shamed a member of his family, a sister or cousin, into including her for the moment.

A loud yell drew her eyes to the tiny window set into the two feet thick outer wall. She could make out, in the sharp sunlight, shapes of small boys moving on the tiny square of communal grass reserved for them. Once she had stood, self-consciously a watcher, for long spells each evening at her window observing the boys. Wullie had shrugged her remarks off, but she thought them a cruel bunch, harder and more vicious than town boys she had been brought up with. Perhaps she had simply never understood them. But she despaired of their sudden cruelties and was secretly relieved that no son of hers had been twisted by the need to 'get on' with his mates.

It had been her and Wullie, just the two of them from the start. And if he had been denied the pride of living through his sons, on summer evenings when the village lads turned out in force to make sides at football, then they had also been spared the wedges which would have been driven between them by having children. Often, as she had stood by her window, she had thought that her love for her own child would have sent her out to the green, wild with anger, to clout the bully who straddled and beat her son about the head. By God, would that have brought the women out in retaliation. But she would have stood by her action. Brutal they were. And thick. Somehow, the village lads seemed more stupid, more insensitive than she could credit.

Then, she would remember that they were bound for the sea, a life of trawl-fishing, and her heart would thump painfully for them. She was more afraid of that roaring, seething, brown mass which heaved up the beach at her in winter and spring than of anything else. In all the years here, she had tried to gain comfort from its presence, to respect and enjoy it. But even Wullie, who had stuck with ship building in preference to the better money to be had at the boats, only ever spoke with pleasure of it when they lay together and listened to the gentle roll of a pacified sea: ''Aye, there's music in that, Mary,'' he'd say, and she would smile in the darkness at his use of her name, a constant reminder that she was not village.

She had been given a woman's name, a saint's name, and was proud of it. How she hated the Jamesinas, the Williaminas, the Georginas, which meant that nearly every woman in the village was called Ina. To distinguish them, the surname was added, another man's name, or their own husband's first name, or their house number, which wasn't theirs but their husband's. Her name was her own, and any daughter of hers would have been called Margaret or Anne, and not been insulted forever by a man's name adopted to keep in mind a disappointment.

And there, of course, she had put her finger on one of the biggest stumbling blocks to acceptance. She hadn't been Chapel, and never could be, though it need never have come to a pitched battle. What a fun they'd had with her, especially on the Feast Days, which took them to work and her to Mass:

"See yon, dressed up to the nines," said Geordie's Bess.

"Aye, but she'll be needin' to pray. Something'll hae tae gie her a hau' to fill that belly of hers," from cousin Ina.

And they'd laughed. The high-pitched, grating cackle had rung in her ears long after she had passed by.

A weak thing in its birth then, this puny religious faith of hers, in the face of village opposition, she had breathed and nursed life into it, until it had developed limbs, a backbone, and finally a brain and had, indeed, filled the cavity of her womb and made her its keeper.

Wullie must have been surprised at her. They had agreed, in courtship, that religion meant little to either of them, so that it didn't amount to an issue. And yet, there she was, stepping out each Sunday, and Holiday of Obligation, and nearly every day in Lent. The only thing he had ever said was:

"You'll be costing me a fortune in Sunday Bests, Lass."

And when she had turned quickly at the door, concerned that he might think her lax in her wifely duties, he had smiled:

"But it's worth it just to see you looking so grand."

A difference in itself that, the Roman Catholic way of making beautiful what they held in reverence. Not for her, the blacks and muted greys of the dour Kirk, the tum-tum-tum of the marching tunes called hymns and praises to God. She had had beauty to fill her mind and soul. Proud words and soaring themes and dreams of betterment had sustained her. Ideas above her station she might well have had, but by God, she had kept them close enough to make the difference.

Yes, she had had her dreams and her aims for life, aims that had never come about. Children aside, since that had been a trial for both her and Wullie, private plans had got lost. She had always wanted to travel, and had somehow thought that in marrying someone so well connected to the sea, she had got half way already to imagined distant shores. She would sit with her back to the fire, on chill evenings, hugging her knees and try to get her husband excited by the pictures she conjured of foreign places remembered from school atlases. She would stretch for and grip his hands, talking up into his face until he laughed:

" What's wrong with good, old Scotland? You'll drive yourself daft with your fancy notions."

She would watch him, once he'd turned back to his newspaper, observe his strong, skilled hands, his lean, muscled arms. He was a builder of boats, a craftsman, and she respected that in him as, in him, she had entrusted her needs and secret hopes. It had been many years past before she had let fade the cherished pictures.

She put her cup in the hearth near her feet and laid her head back on the chair. Those story shapes she had made had flitted in and out of her head, stirring her emotions and filling up her life. Such colours. Even in Church, or on the bus there and back, her mind in those days would be away in amongst the shapes, till she turned the handle of her own front door, or Wullie asked:

"Well, have you done with sin for another week?"

Then, with a start, she would realise that she hadn't taken in a word the priest had said, and that the Mass had passed like a silent tableau, as far as improving her mind was concerned.

Wullie had been right, the pictures and dreams had sometimes frustrated her; but he had been wrong in thinking that she could be without them. There was that story she had once read, which she could clearly recall, about a woman not unlike herself who had been brought into a close community by marriage. That woman was hounded personally, through her children, and by her husband's countless infidelities until, half demented by the mysterious death of her youngest child, she threw herself, embittered and in despair, under the hooves of the chief's horse.

She'd been stopped in her tracks by that story, and had slowly and painfully unravelled the threads of bitterness in her mind, till she was left with the cold steel of pure anger. Then, with eyes to the fore, she had continued on her way.

She rolled her head gently on the hard back of the chair. No, she had lost nothing with the disappearance of the dreams: she'd just slowly let go of them, allowed time, and no person, to sap their strength. Like her religion. Once the village, years on, had accepted her right to her own beliefs, then left to itself, the poor thing, that was her faith, had rattled its bones at her and departed.

"Hullo. Are you there? It's me."

The letter-box clattered as she opened her eyes:

"Aye, I'm here. Come away in." She heard the familiar, heavy tread in her lobby and pulled herself into a more upright position in the armchair. Ina's face appeared round the side of the door:

"Are you needing milk, Wifie. I know fine that mine's aff."

The mobile grocer's van must have arrived. She was surprised that she hadn't noticed the toot-tooting of his horn.

"Och, it's that time already! I was just having forty winks."

She moved forward on her seat, bending her arms on the sides to lever herself up. The effort suddenly seemed too much and she let herself fall gently back into it.

"You're alright?" Ina had taken a couple of steps into the room. She noticed, with irritation, that Ina's face wore an expression of concern.

"Of course I'm OK. It's just the damned heat."

"You don't look yourself. A funny colour."

"I'm fine I tell you. You're nae sae bonny yerself." She was going to have to get up; the matter wouldn't be dropped.

"Hand me my purse down. I'll take half a pint."

Ina turned in the direction of her nod, and she took the chance to slide her behind to the very edge of the seat. By the time Ina was stretching the purse forward, she was on her feet, smiling:

"Technique," she said with a gasping laugh. "I mustna lose the knack."

"A half pint you say?" Ina was still boring her eyes home.

"Aye. And I've my order to get. Just a small plain. He kens. Tell him it's for Mary." She stressed the point.

Ina was backing away from her, towards the door.

"And if you just leave it on the step. I'm going out."

The door clicked to.

"Nosey, damned bitch," she muttered. Ina, Georgina, Geordie's Jamie's Ina, her

T-name no more distinguished than her christening one, she thought her blood ties with Wullie gave her a special privilege to ask direct questions. She was always insinuating herself. There was no getting through to some folk. "There's naen sae blind . . .," she mumbled aloud, and tilted her chin to see herself better in the mirror. Maybe her face was a bit high-coloured. So what! How was anybody's face in this freak heat. Ina had always been quick to point out her shortcomings, though she was better at it behind a body's back. She had caught the bitch, redhanded, making her out to be not quite up to the mark - to Wullie. Unmarried herself, she had early latched onto the young couple, her cousin Wullie and his wifie, for visits and acts of friendship, so long as no one was looking.

Then, one evening, warned in advance that it wasn't convenient, Ina had appeared at the kitchen door pretending surprise at the Sunday clothes.
"Oh, I'm right sorry to catch you going out. I'd thought we might look the paper together."
"Well I've Church. Confession."
Wullie, at the fireside, nodded at her, and turned back to his football coupon. She didn't want to be rude to her only visitor, but neither did she want to leave her there:
"I'm just on my way. Do you feel like a walk to the bus?"
Ina moved to the other fireside chair and sat down with a groan:
"Oh, my feet. Standing all day at thae barrels. My corns are fair dinging. No that I'll bide lang." Ina smiled up at her.
"I'd better be off then, for that bus." She turned to Wullie, undecided.
"I'll have the kettle on," he said.

She had gone then, dragging her feet, and watched with a bad conscience, the back of the bus disappearing up the long, cobbled street towards the town.
"That's her fault," she said, but her heart was thumping with dread rather than anger when she crept into the house.

And there it was, the veiled criticism. No more than had been said to her face: "Queer kind of religion th'on. The kind of thing foreigners do," and so on, with never a word from Wullie.
"I missed it," she said, thumping her handbag down on the sideboard.
"And now if you'll just leave us together, Ina, I'll get my husband his supper."
Ina had scurried then, red in the face, hadn't come back and never been invited. Not for years. But she had been hurt. And with the relief of finding Wullie innocently at his coupons, she had burst into tears. Which had been sorted out easily enough, with Wullie's arm round her shoulder:
"I know fine you're different. I married you for it. I don't need any scaly besom to point it out." And she had laughed and cried at the same time; laughed for his love and cried for this and all the betrayals she could look forward to.

But that was long past, and now she would even let Ina fetch milk sometimes and not resent it. Though her heart was hammering at bringing it all back. She would go out. She had said she would. A stroll on the beach for old times' sake. She rolled her stockings up past her knees, retied her apron and patted her hair.

There wasn't a breath of wind as she headed round the end of the row and on down the boat-launching slip to the sandy beach. The sweat was drying on her face, but her back between her shoulder blades, was damp. Her feet sank deep into the sand. There was not a soul in sight, not even some kids, although she could hear sharp voices raised from somewhere close, out of sight.

It was no longer clear to her why she had come, for the effort to pull one foot up and past the other was causing the breath to strain in her chest. Then she remembered the acute pleasure of paddling in the sea and she made for the pier which supported the first in a series of lighthouses. She had a vivid picture of a shallow pool between rocks where she would sit, stockings off, and dangle her feet. She concentrated on keeping her sucked-on slippers moving forward, listening to her rattling breath, and glanced across the shimmering water to where? Norway she had always supposed. Fjords, fir trees and dour folk, like the Scots. Another place she would never go to.

She stretched out both hands and felt the comforting roughness of dry rock. Bent forward she drew deep breaths, the sun beating on her head and back. Nearly there. She wouldn't go back until her feet were good and paddled. She shook her head: ''You're a stupid, old woman,'' she told herself. ''No better than the stupid folk you've spent your life with, for all your fancy notions. Travel. Hah. All that sea and never the means.''

With faltering steps, she eased her bulk round and between rocks, until she realised that there were no pools: they had been dried up by the sun. She looked towards the sea with barely a ripple on it. White light danced for her as she blinked away. A few more yards and she could sit over there on a peninsula, far enough out for anyone. She felt her way forward, hands curled on shiny rock growths, till she stood at the very edge, staring down into a good six feet of water. She had made it. She smiled down into the clear, deep pool, all fear slipping from her.

She twisted her head round to see how far she had come and the pain, sharp as a man's punch, hit her in the chest. She gasped, clutched sideways at air and felt her body become suddenly weightless. As her head broke the flat surface, the deliciously cool water held her eyelids shut.

Rosemary Mackay

# DOWN

It was when I saw Madge at the other end of the playground that I first thought: "Dear God." It wasn't one of those unbidden, spontaneous curses which can ring, in sporadic bursts, throughout an entire day, no spur quite connected to the next. This was a considered blasphemy and in those two words there was a weight of disgust great enough to sink a steamship.

"Dear God", I thought and realised that my knowledge of Madge, won over twenty years of my life, went for nothing. Try as I might, and I might have to, it would be impossible for me, for anyone, to give Madge a good character.

There had been the complaint from outside, there had been confirmation from inside, and now here was Madge, scurrying off, head bent, possibly into the wind and against the lashing rain, but also bent, to all intents and purposes, in shame; and as I drew the thin curtains across my classroom window, against the sight of the vanishing light, for the third time, I thought:

"Dear God."

I turned slowly on the class, their young heads bowed at work, except for one: she had caught me, her soft, brown eyes ovalled, trying to read my face, while puberty had already thrown her instincts off. She adored me, like half a dozen others in the class, would follow me anywhere. But the acknowledgement of this had the force to drag me down, instead of the routine uplifting of twenty-five years of the dedication of my pupils and I knew what had happened to Madge, the beginning of the slide. At that moment, the small face not ten feet from me, coloured, the eyes moist as the head went down and I had another situation to resolve, a cause to champion, a heart and mind to cosset and lead.

"Right. Enough," I bawled. "You've worked quite hard enough. Julie." The brown eyes flashed in expectation: already, I was forgiven for my indelicacy. "Collect in the text-books. Hand out some drawing-paper. There's fifteen minutes left. Draw me a picture of the central incident in the story. Now then, what was there? George, your hand's up. Yes, a cat. Billy, your hand is not up. Yes . . .?"

As the calm atmosphere moved through mayhem to relaxed, contented activity, I sat at my desk and began to shuffle through the papers before me, intent on remembering that half-hour in the staffroom, less than a year ago.

"I don't know," said Madge, "sometimes I feel that in the end, in the final analysis, we let them down."

"Whom?" I fitted my teacup into the small space between my crossword and a pile of homework jotters on the coffee table which nudged my knees each time I moved and dragged my eyes across to Madge. There was only ten minutes left of my single free period of the week and Madge wanted to take it from me. But the droop of her shoulders, the anxious twist to her mouth, shocked me into participation. Madge shook her head quickly and glanced down at her ringless hands which tugged at a button on her cardigan.

"Sorry. Just speaking aloud. Finish your crossword, Alex."

"Now Madge, when did I ever ignore an opening like that? Come on now, tell your Uncle Alex all about it."

The youngish PE teacher, the single other occupant of the staffroom, who was sitting quite near us, gave a snorting laugh and Madge twitched her shoulders round, the better to shut him out. I gave her my second-gentlest smile and raised my eyebrows. She wrinkled her nose at me and said:

"Oh, it's just the same old thing, the merry-go-round. Here we are, ready, as soon as the Highers are over, to shunt them all out into that dreadful society of ours and I feel that it's so cruel, that they're so young and ill-equipped . . ." she caught my grimace, but rushed on:

"I know all that, Alex. I know what our job is. But when they come to you with their brave, little smiles and ask for more and all we can do is fob them off with meaningless remarks about how good their prospects are. . . ."

"Ask for what? Madge, what are you reading into this? Your own projections . . ." I asked this kindly, though uncomfortable with the imposed role of counsellor.

"I know what they think they're asking for and I know what they're actually asking for and the two don't match." The PE chap, whose name I never remember, spoke loudly, too loudly and as Madge and I looked at him, he made a gesture of drawing one forearm up sharply towards the ceiling while smacking his straining bicep with his free hand. I watched Madge give him one of her renowned withering stares, waiting until she turned back to me before I said quietly:

"Do you have someone specific in mind, Miss Taylor, or are you making a general comment?" I gave her the formal title as a suggestion to our eavesdropper that such rubbishing was not appropriate; but Madge misunderstood and the lines of her face set in their professional mode.

"Look, Madge, if you want to speak to me in private . . . I know that class well. If you want me to come and talk to them, sort something out. I mean, the career prospects can be covered and . . ."

"Nothing to sort out, Alex. I'm just letting off steam, thank you."

I gazed at her, but her stony expression mirrored her feelings exactly. As the bell ripped through the silence I said:

"OK, Madge. But keep me in mind, eh?"

"Billeeee. Drawing, my lad, not chatting up the girls."

The wee boy blushed suitably in the burst of laughter from the class and I let my mind go back.

It was so difficult to sort out the next few weeks following that abortive scene with Madge, amidst the frantic organising then marking of exam papers characteristic of that phase of the teaching year, although I could recall now snatches of Madge's deepening tension and misery. She lost weight, so rapidly that a rumour soon emerged that she was dying from cancer. As her Head of Department, I let the claim go by me: Madge could be relied on, before anyone, to communicate officially any intended termination of her contract. However, as the clothes began to hang on her, as her normally spruce appearance began to dry out and yellow, I wondered if she was the same Madge I had worked with for so long. Then suddenly, the change.

I had gone to her classroom one day, once the final bell had gone, to ask about some administrative detail and as I approached her classroom, Mary Bell, a dark haired, blue-eyed beauty in Fifth Year, rushed out past me, with a radiant smile:

"Bye, Sir," she said.

"Good afternoon, Mary," I nodded her passing, then stopped in Madge's doorway.

She was seated at her desk, head in hands, her shoulders shaking and a cold dread of some final collapse filled me. But Mary's face didn't fit with Madge's distress, unless there was some crusade against Madge being perpetrated. I walked quickly towards the desk:

"Madge, are you alright? Madge!"

Madge raised a tear-streaked face towards me, her mouth ugly with emotion, snot rattling in her sinuses:

"I'm fine. Fine. Sorry." She blew her nose noisily on the kleenex I handed her. "I'm fine, fine." She was shaking her head, trying on a smile:

"Mary's staying on, for a sixth year, despite the fact that I've warned her that Universities don't encourage it. We'll be OK, fine." Her eyes sparkled at me, possibly because of the tears, and my heart sank a little further.

"Madge, if this is all getting too much for you, there is secondment, a year away from all this stress. I would miss you, but really, in the long term. . . ."

"No." Madge was definite, the shadow of her former strength and decisiveness returning. "I might consider it for the year after. I wouldn't miss next year if they doubled my wages, trebled them. Now, is there something I can do for you?"

Apart from the blotches, her face was composed and I let it all go. I could see that now, sitting here watching the print before me blur and focus, blur and focus. I should have been firm, insisted that she go. I should have known. I should have had the scrap of imagination necessary to feel her loneliness. But there's knowing and knowing, knowing and not-knowing. I wanted Madge to be happy, but I chose to unknow the source.

It wasn't as if there were no signs, signals almost, facial expressions which challenged and finally dared a reaction. I'd met them once myself, one lunchtime in the next teaching year, Madge locking the store-room door, while the other, Mary, giggled and me calling and Madge's defiance, through the haze of joy in her eyes.

"I want a word, Mr Murdoch," this from Jeff, the Head of Maths, his expression stern, the grey eyebrows a jagged line.

"About a member of your staff, Miss Taylor. I saw her in the theatre bar last night, in the company of a pupil, and if their glasses held only orange juice, then I'm a Dutchman."

"It's not unusual, Jeff, especially in the Sixth Year, for cultural trips . . ."

"Singly? Just a word of warning, Alex, a friendly word in the ear, to be passed on, as you see fit, of course."

And I didn't: the knowing and not-knowing; the fear between.

"Right, that's it. Pack up your things. And try not to bang your desk, Tommy . . . File out."

The bell pealed through their uproar.

"Slowly," I yelled.

"Mr Murdoch?" a quiet presence at my side.

"Yes, Julie."

"It's the final part of that serial tonight I was telling you about. I thought . . ."

"Yes, I'll watch it, Julie." I smiled, slightly to the left of her face. "We'll try to get a class discussion on it on Monday. Have a good weekend."

"And you."

Her small frame followed the stragglers out and the sight of her pale, thin legs stretching from the hem of her skirt to the tops of her short, white socks made me turn my eyes quickly away.

"Poor sods," I thought. "Poor little sods."

My own children had been through it all and I understood exactly their conflict, the confusion in their own heads which informed the mixed messages they gave. I saw again Madge's cowed figure, Madge who had not understood this about them and who would not be understood in her turn. She was ruined, disgrace heaped upon disgrace, until no one hanged in the last centuries died with more on her conscience than Madge had. She was down; down and out.

"Dear God," I said aloud.

Rosemary Mackay

# THE WEDDING DAY

So there I was, sat in the tin tub, before the dead, bedroom fireplace, feeling the water going cold, staring at the goose pimples on my thighs. I was bolt upright, in one of the two possible positions and my bent-up knees were a hair's beadth from the tip of my nose. In that position there was no problem about where the soap was: the only space was behind my ankles, next to my bum. I thought about asking my Mother to come and wash my back, decided that the odds were not in my favour, and manoeuvred my feet out of the bath and onto the linoleum. From there, I eased my bum forward, careful to avoid contact with the base grit which ripped soft flesh. Very gently and slowly, keeping firmly in mind the handle of the tub which jutted from the rim, I leant back until the top of my spine was touching the inside of the tub and my chin was wedged on my chest. Now the soap had to be in the triangle between spine and tub, unreachable.

I eyed the scum which was lapping around my crevices, and reckoned that my back done, my conscience was clear. That made two baths in one week. Would Lizzie have done as much for my wedding? I asked myself. The front door opened and I heard my sisters' laughter as they entered the living room. They had time to go to the Public Baths: but my paper round stopped me. Heaven and earth might pass away, but that bloody paper round would go on and on. I sighed, heard myself sighing, and began the business of drawing my body into an upright position. My feet, still on the linoleum, were freezing.

It was a farce, the whole bloody business. Here was Lizzie, saving all her earnings for two whole years to pay for the White Wedding, the Cathedral Service with Nuptial Mass, the big Reception in the best Hotel in town, and every relative we possessed, who had not spoken to any of us in years and would not speak again after today, invited to attend. They would be there: they couldn't resist the temptation of the gilt-edged Invitation Card. But they were coming in the hope of catching us out, we, the lower-class end of the family.

And the fiancée. Well, my God, wasn't he a corker. Hamish, who spoke through a mouthful of marbles, and could be seen, his neighbours had said, sporting the old school tie as he dug his patch. Certainly, he had never crossed our threshold: all social niceties had been performed in the lobby, no matter the time of day or temperature. I had amused myself speculating on how to get Hamish out to the back garden where he could be invited to ''avail himself of our facilities''. But Lizzie roused, had a hell of a punch on her, and could kick like a kangaroo.

I towel-dried the goose pimples away, deciding that I would put on the new underclothes now, but I'd be damned if I was going to wear that dress before it was absolutely necessary. Not that you could hope to stand on principle in a farce. That had been made quite clear when Mother started acting up in the shoe shop. Which had nothing to do with anything I had said: she was just overwrought by her own finer feelings. That and the heat, and the quarrelling and the dirty looks we were getting from the shop assistant.

But there was still two hours till the show got on the road, and dressed in that crazy rig-out, I would not be able to do the fetching and carrying, accept my ''delegated responsibilities'', as Lizzie called them. She would persist in treating me as though I was as gullible as the rest, though you could tell sometimes from her face that she wasn't getting the same satisfaction, the cheeky bitch. I pulled on my dirty jeans and went to meet what had to be the last in a life-time of tantrums from my older sister.

Lizzie was standing in the middle of the living room floor, arms aloft supporting umpteen rolls of white material, face livid as she hissed at her sisters:
"Get a hold on either side, you gormless buggers. It weighs a ton."
I had never before been favoured with a full frontal of my sister, even half-clothed, since we all four got ourselves into contortions trying to avoid the casual glance, as we wrestled into pyjamas, bras, knickers. Life was simpler in behind the clothes-horse, but when the horse was up, there was no room for anyone else to move. Now, as the descending hem line concealed first, a scattering of plooks, then the chalk-white midriff, next the sprouting pubic hair, and finally a small ladder in one stocking, I recognised that cover had its advantages.

"What are you gawping at? And what the hell kept you? Get the zip." It was a beautiful dress; I had to admit it. But I couldn't understand why it was going on now, with the rollers and naked face above it. I knew I could rely on one of my sisters to do the necessary:
"Why are you putting it on now, Lizzie?" asked Jessie.
"Why the hell do you think? Get a hold of the train, carefully. And get a chair. I'm wanting to have a look."

In procession, we moved slowly to the positioned chair, which Lizzie gingerly mounted. The mirror, which was eight inches by eight inches, reflected Lizzie's splendidly-clad stomach.
"Hold the train back," she said and slowly began to bend her knees until she could see her own neck line. Then, centimetre by centimetre, she straightened her knees until she could see her midriff again. Now, she went on tip-toe, craning up until she got a view at knee height:
"Jesus, this is just a bloody game."
"My sentiments, exactly," I offered, and received a stinging slap on the side of my head.
"And who bloody asked you?" she said. I gave her one of my winning smiles and wondered where on earth Mother had gone.

Lizzie stepped off the chair, and the train was placed at her ankles:
"Get me something to protect the dress. A tea-cloth or something to catch the powder. And for God's sake start getting ready. Jessie, Ellen. Move it."
I draped a tablecloth round her shoulders, pinning it at the back: "Anything else?" I said. "Where's your make up?" I knew she would do a great job on her face. Any night of the week she could swan out of there looking like one of the jet-set.
"I'm fine. See to yourself." She tossed a powder compact at me which I took to be for my personal use. In the mirror of this contraption, you could see two whole square inches of your face at a time. I propped it against the milk jug and sat down at the table.

The door opened and Mother came in with her coat and head-square on:
"Uncle Jimmy wasn't in, but Auntie Maisie says everything is under control, and he'll be along at twelve."

"Oh, where's he then? Down at the pub?" I threw Mother's flushed face a glance and she shook her head vigorously at me.

"Oh Jesus," I thought. "That's all we're needing."

"How's he getting here?" asked Lizzie.

"They've got a taxi ordered." Presumably in case he couldn't walk. Mother disappeared into the bedroom carrying a basin of hot water. There was no time now for an all-over effort.

I concentrated on my right eye, pulling the eye-liner pencil as firmly as I could across the puckering, flesh. For years, I had watched Lizzie do this with the total concentration of an artist. And though I could applaud her finished efforts, I remained unconvinced where my own mask was concerned. What, after all, was it for? The outside world, as far as I knew, was unmoved by my efforts. I spat into the cracked cake of mascarra, and rubbed the clogged, solid bristles of my brush, spittle-covered, on the black, resisting block. I had tried to stand my ground on this issue too, sidling past the waiting Lizzie in my Sunday clothes, barefaced but scrubbed clean. The sneer she gave me then, had me reaching for the make-up bag before I had time to register a change of mind.

I opened my eye as wide as possible and with trembling hand waved the loaded brush at my flickering eyelashes. The roar which came from the bedroom sent the brush flying across the table, and my body into collision with Lizzie's in the doorway.

"Jesus God. Jesus, help me."

My mother was lying on her back across the bed, breasts and open mouth reaching for the ceiling, her vast corset packed tight. She was waving her arms and a loud sob escaped from her throat.

"What the hell is it?" Lizzie stood over her, staring down at the purpling face. My mother's left hand made an arc and her fingers began to scrabble at the reinforced cotton of her corset. It was done up to midway and then gaped obscenely at her navel. Beneath this, I noticed tiny mounds of blue flesh poking through at the join: she was trapped.

At that moment, Lizzie flung the tablecloth from around her neck and began to force open the hooks and eyes which trapped the purple bumps. My mother let out a scream and pulled her knees up towards her belly. It was then that I saw the cord which was laced to draw the front of the corset together.

"A pair of scissors," I said as I rushed to the sideboard drawer. There was everything but.

"A knife," I said. Mother's screams were making my stomach cramp. I knew the carver was as blunt as a spade and so I whipped up the breadknife. Back in the bedroom, I began to saw at the cord, glad that I had something to do, trying to shut out the now white face, the dying sobs. When the last thread snapped, my mother's arched torso slumped. Lizzie unhooked the lumps and my mother let out a final groan.

"And that had better be the last thing I ever do in this bloody madhouse. Mary, my train." Lizzie snatched up her tablecloth and, in procession, we left the bedroom.

And then we had to go; me, Mother, Jessie and Ellen in one taxi, and Uncle Jimmy, in striped trousers and tails, weaving in the doorway, his nose already changing colour. Lizzie, majestic in veil, had taken one look at his leering face and swept past him into the bedroom, Ellen pursuing the flicking train.

"Aye, it's good to see you, James. You're looking very nice." My Mother always treated drunks with patient good humour, and I could never see the point. "Aye, the girls are looking lovely," she responded to his grin at me and Jessie. "We're away now. Your taxi will be in five minutes. Take care."

"My God, could he not have just this once laid off . . ."

Our own father had gone off in a binge four years before and hadn't been seen since. So Jimmy, Mother's brother, stood in when necessary.

"Now, don't go on, Mary," said Mother. "He's just behaving the way he always does for weddings."

"But he's giving her away, for God's sake. He'll be staggering down the aisle."

"Don't underestimate him. He's had plenty of practise. And don't go on. Is my flower straight?"

She patted the spray above her left breast:

"I think they've made a lovely job of the flowers, don't you?" She stroked her stomach and winced.

Now that we were away from the house, my younger sisters were exploding with laughter next to my Mother.

"Calm down, you two. You're flower girls. Behave like it."

I sat in the front seat, clutching a pink posy, desperate at the thought that I couldn't expect a fag until the Reception. Then I remembered my Mother's handbag: "Light a fag, Mother, I'm gasping."

"You can't, Mary. Not dressed like that."

"Look Mother, if Uncle Jimmy can turn up pissed out of his brains, then I can smoke a fag."

"Ssh," she said with headjerk at the taxi driver, who showed an impassive profile. She lit the cigarette, taking three quick draws on it, in her infuriating way, and passed it to me.

Mother went in to take her seat, and we stood in the Church vestibule waiting for Lizzie, from where I could see the seated congregation, resplendent in fur stoles and huge hats. And we hadn't even had an autumn frost yet. Suddenly, Mother burst through the glass doors, her eyes frantic: "He's not here. God Almighty. He hasn't turned up." She was trying to whisper, but seemed to have little control of her voice.

"Who, the Minister?"

"No. That bloody Hamish!" Mother had, to date, spoken of him only in neutral terms.

"Well, she's not here either."

"But he's supposed to be. Dear God, what if he's jilted her?" And what if he had? Wouldn't that be the last laugh for the guests? "The McIvies have done it again. Another glorious cock-up." I could hear them all at it. Not that we ever had done the like before. But it was easy to establish a tradition in inferiority, if the will was there. I'd kill him if he had let us down.

Mother pulled her head back in the front door: "Lizzie's here. I'll have to go and tell her. They'll hold everything for a while." She disappeared again, and I became conscious of the sweat gathering in my armpits. My little sisters looked stricken.

"Come on," I said. "It could be the best thing that's happened to her."
"But I'm affronted," said Ellen, and her lower lip began to wobble.
"Don't you dare greet," I said. I wanted to go into the pulpit, mount a machine gun, and mow the congregation down.

Through the glass doors, I could see heads slowly turning, then moving together for whispered messages. Feet were beginning to shuffle. "It's alright, you'll get your bloody presents back," I wanted to scream. Instead, I moved to the door and opened it. Mother was tripping across the street, knees pushing her dress forward, hat slightly askew. Behind her, I could see Lizzie's taxi. Even Uncle Jimmy's face seemed to have gone a few shades paler. Lizzie shouldn't have to take this. I felt a surge of loyal pity that almost choked me.

And then, there he was. With a great roaring of engine and screeching of brakes, he leapt out of the roofless sports car, and loped towards me, a flop of blonde hair across one eye.
"Where the hell have you been?" I hissed.
His best man burst in behind him and my words were lost. Within minutes they had struck up 'Here Comes The Bride', and for one terrifying moment, I thought I was going to let the side down and shed a tear.

Rosemary Mackay

# A STORY WITHOUT SENSE

Ellen had climbed up behind the corrugated iron sheets stacked in the playground shelter, and hidden there, smiling in the near-dark. Though it was the only really good spot left, no one else had dared to go. She crouched and remembered other hiding places, better with a pal, in the woods, ducked down in the broken-off trunk of a tree, crunching wood lice and beetles underfoot, giggling silently.

She could hear the shouts as school mates outran the 'man' to the dell, the slap of feet on concrete as they sped past. And then, the hand-bell clanging to sound the end of lunch break. Ellen crawled backwards out of the small space between sheeting and brick, jumped down and ran squinting into the sunlight. She clapped the 'man' on the back as she passed her:

"Didn't get me," she gasped.

"You were out of the playground. Cheat!" shouted Kath, her sister, catching up and throwing an arm round Ellen's neck. Ellen wriggled free laughing, and jostled Kath into the doorway.

"I'm not a cheat. You're just a useless man."

"Where were you, then?" asked Matty.

"Why? So you can try it next time? Huh! Scaredy-cat." She laughed back at him down the stairs. Then, they were on the landing, and she could see, through the metal uprights of the banister, the edge of black hem, the two black shoes.

The nun was waiting outside her office, at the top of the stairs, again. Ellen panicked and pushed Matty aside, trying to get back down against the tide of bodies. "Hey! Watch it!"

She looked down over the heads of children, but too late: the teacher, hand-bell stilled, was on her way up. Someone tugged her arm.

"Hey, Elly, what's the matter?" She was being forced sideways and back, out of the mainstream. Any further and she'd be visible from the head of the stairs. She grasped her sister's hand.

"She's waiting."

"Again! Quick, get behind me, into the wall."

Sucked back in, they climbed. Don't look at her. Just don't let her catch your eye. She won't call. If she doesn't see you, she won't even think of it. Three stairs to go, head down, Ellen stared at the back of her sister's cardigan, a pulled thread with a tuft of wool two-thirds of the way down it. Her mouth was dry, her calf muscles trembling. One, two, three: and light streamed from the open classroom door. She put her head up to gulp air.

"Ellen Fraser!"

Oh God. Oh Jesus, Mary and Joseph.

Ellen's step faltered. Her sister's hand shot behind her back and tugged Ellen's sleeve. She could dare to go on, as though she hadn't heard: but then . . . Her mind closed. She stopped and someone crashed into her, pushing her into the door jamb, as they stumbled past. Ellen began to smile and turned:

"Yes, Mother?"

The thin, white face was tight, framed by an oval wimple. The nun caught the loose edge of her black veil at the neck -- *Ellen, your attitude is all wrong* -- and with a jerk of the head - *you're not a good influence on others* - flicked the veil back over one shoulder, her mouth pinched in irritation. She gestured Ellen to stand by her side. Unconcerned heads bobbed below and up past Ellen. She was one of them, should be seated by now, getting out her books, calling to her friends. A boy tripped on the end of a long, tubular screen, where it lay on the floor by the wall, school projector next to it. Help with carrying that. That was all. Ellen shot a glance up at the nun's face, encouraging the words of command:

"Wait at my door," she said, without a downward flicker of her eyes. Ellen, still smiling, inclined her head, as they had been taught to do at shrines and statues, and turned into the short, dark corridor which was the entrance to the Headmistress's office.

Every day. Every day for a week. And lots of times before that. Standing in there. Being talked at, on and on: words that went round and round. Like scribbles on a page. *Not like the other children. Different. Why are you different, Ellen? I'm trying to understand you.* And the eyes boring into her.

The flow of bodies was becoming a trickle. Ellen stood in the darkness and stared at the place where her feet should be, aware that she was panting. She dragged her palms down her thighs and swallowed hard on the lump in her throat, no spit to gather. After a while, in the office, breathing became difficult. It was a stuffy, horrible room. But she must smile. Whatever was said, she mustn't stop smiling. Sticks and stones . . . The Staff Room door above and beyond the nun's shape opened noisily and a blond-grey head appeared, in tight curls, wreathed in smoke, closely followed by a large, fat body.

At the sight of her own teacher, Ellen pushed herself off the wall and began to slap her hands at her sides. She craned her neck, poking her face towards the light. She cursed her dark clothes. Even a pair of white socks would have helped. The teacher rumbled down the few steps to the landing, where the nun stood.

"Good afternoon, Mrs Ritchie," the black head nodded sharply.

"Good afternoon, Mother Morran." Mrs Ritchie had stopped to wrestle with a pile of books in her arms. She turned and peered towards Ellen.

"Oh God, please," Ellen shuffled her feet.

Mrs Ritchie walked away, and the nun swooped down to her office.

They stood together in the tiny space, the nun fumbling with a pile of keys at her belted waist, Ellen pressed back against the wall, in dread of the touch of her habit. The door opened, and the nun entered the small, overfurnished room. A skylight on the sloped ceiling spilled a square of sunshine across her desk; the only other window, high up on the outside wall, had frosted glass which broke up the light.

"Come in, Ellen."

Ellen pulled her mouth back into a smile and stepped across the threshold.

"Shut the door." The nun sat and began moving papers around on her desk. Ellen positioned herself opposite. There was nowhere to look except at the nun. She thought of nothing, stiffly waiting. Then, the shuffling of papers stopped. The nun pushed a hand inside her bodice, and produced a large, gent's watch. She flipped the lid, stared for a moment at the watch face, then snapped the lid shut. Ellen's body twitched and the nun looked up quickly into her face. Ellen chose a point four inches above the nun's head and smiled at it.

"Ellen, look at me."

She sat just beyond the shaft of sunlight, momentarily lost to sight, till the stark, white face took shape. She had the palest eyes that Ellen knew of, with tiny, red veins at the extreme edges. Ellen fixed on the bridge of her nose.

"Well then . . ." she suggested.

Ellen shifted onto one foot and locked the hip. Her hands were clasped wetly behind her back and she concentrated on her balance. She lifted her shoulders in a shrug and smiled, wider. The white face moved, the mouth opened, closed almost soft:

"Just as you wish, Ellen."

The nun scraped her chair back from the desk, the black garments rolled in rigid folds, the veil collapsed sideways in a head tilt. The large, silver cross moved off the nun's flat chest and swung free. An arm flapped out, crooked, a bony, white hand curled at the end. Ellen moved her head to see, following the direction of the pointing hand. She turned back to the nun, questioning.

"Round here, Ellen. Come round."

Ellen thought hard about the manoeuvre, giving suddenly onto the other foot and willed her body round and forward, towards the nun. The nun's arm went tight round her waist and Ellen looked quickly into and away from the grey eyes, the nun's breath already enclosing her.

"That's better, isn't it? Close like this?"

Ellen dropped her head, slowly raised it.

"I have a story that I want to tell you."

Ellen watched the dust motes dancing in the sunlight. What fun to stretch and catch them; to search for them in the palm of her hand and throw them, invisible, back into the light.

"A story about a young nun who became a saint."

Ellen turned her eyes to a picture on the opposite wall. Jesus with children, birds wooden on the ground, lambs hewn out of marble: the words at the foot of the picture said, "Suffer the little children to come unto me."

"This young saint was so good, so holy and so young, that not everyone in the Convent liked her. Some of her sisters in Christ were jealous of her goodness, and one of them tried to stop her being good by teasing her all the time."

Ellen slowly gripped her skirt at the thighs and wrung out her hands. Children shouldn't suffer to go to Jesus. Or Jesus shouldn't suffer because of the children. The picture dimmed and shifted. A hard blink brought Jesus' bearded-woman's face clear. Ellen's knee-caps were quivering. She bent one leg and leant out of the nun's embrace. The arm tightened on her waist.

"One day, the jealous sister-nun began to splash water into the saint's face while they were together, washing clothes at a sink. The saint did nothing. She wasn't supposed to speak anyway. A Rule of Silence. Her sister-nun splashed more water. But, for the saint, it was as if it wasn't happening." The nun leant forward, twisting her head to look up into Ellen's face. A musty smell of air-starved clothes rose into Ellen's nostrils. She turned to the red-veined eyes, slowly craning her head back as she did so. The dust particles danced higher, momentarily frenzied, then drifted. Up in the skylight, dead blue-bottles dangled. Suffer the little children, suffer the children. Ellen's face ached with her smile, her mind seeming to float inches above her head.

"The saint didn't know why the nun disliked her. So she prayed harder for understanding. She prayed for the nun, and she prayed to God to take her into Heaven."

Jesus, Mary and Joseph, I give you my heart and my soul. Jesus, Mary and Joseph, I place my trust in Thee. Jesus, let me go.

The nun moved her arm suddenly from Ellen's waist, and Ellen staggered backwards two, three steps: stopped. The nun stared at her. Ellen felt hot all over. The sweat broke on her neck, face and backs of knees. She took a hesitant step forward. The grey eyes were hard.

"The saint knew humility. She knew love. And she loved God and goodness more than anything. Ellen, why do you smile all the time?"

Ellen shrugged, shuffled her feet, looked round at the circular, opaque window above her head.

"It's not a nice smile, Ellen. And it doesn't make you look very pretty."

Ellen opened her mouth to speak and the words, sharp and quick for a second, drifted away.

"Yes? Yes! What is it, Ellen?"

"I've forgotten." She smiled easily. It was true. She had nothing to say. The story was finished. A story without sense.

"Forgotten! You expect me to believe that silliness? Forgotten. Well, we'll see." The nun gathered her long skirts in one hand and turned her body away from Ellen's.

"Tell Mrs Ritchie you were with me. Go."

"Thank-you, Mother." Ellen curtsied, walked quickly to the door and closed it behind her.

In the dense passage, she dropped her eyes to the darkness at her feet, easing off her neck. She was desperate to go to the toilet, but would have had to ask the nun's permission to go. She walked through the Primary Four and Five classroom and into her own.

"And where this time?" bawled Mrs Ritchie, who was leaning against the only radiator, book in hand.

"With Mother Morran." Ellen didn't look at her, or at her sister's anxious face over in the Primary Seven rows. She sat down and drew her finger along the familiar, etched grooves on her desk-top. She wanted, more than anything, to sleep.

"Oh, very cosy. Just the two of you. Again." Some of the children giggled.

"You come in here, as bold as brass, disrupting my class, ready to make trouble. But I know the weepings and wailings that go on."

Weepings. Crying. Ellen looked round at the faces. They all showed surprise. A few sniggered.

"Not crying. I don't cry. I wouldn't!"

Through her rage, Ellen saw Mrs Ritchie's face change. Something. Some question. Then she realised that she had stood up. She flicked the seat down into a crash and sat. She knew what her sister's face would say, so she stared at the blackboard-shapes.

"Matthew McHugh, go and sit next to her and share your book. Now that she's here, she might as well join in the work of the class.''

Ellen put up her hand:

''Please. I need to go to the toilet.''

''Well, you've wasted enough of my time already. If you still need by the end of English ask then.''

Ellen crossed her legs and turned to Matty. He smelled sour and his teeth were stained. He was the thickest pupil in the class. Ellen moved closer to him and bent her head to his.

Rosemary Mackay

# INTRUSIONS

"Come on, come on, come on," Maggie set her feet lashing the air, an inch from the floor and rubbed vigorously at her thighs. Then she shivered convulsively and bit her tongue. Tears sprang to her eyes; the back of the door, less than three feet from her face, wavered dimly. She jerked her head back to stare up at the tiny, frosted-glass window above her head, trying to judge, by the vanishing light, how long she had been sitting there. At least there were no spiders to plague her this time of year, though the tenants were bound to install a paraffin heater soon to avoid the expense of a freeze-up. Then she would have to sit further forward so that the condensation didn't drip on her back.

She cast her eyes to the patches where the plaster had crumbled off the walls, to the flaking pink paint which exposed an ugly brown, like the shade on the door and she surveyed her animal companions: there was the lion with his stiff mane, there the dog in flight, there the noble elegance of a cat. But what was the shape down there by the door-post? Her mind winced from the image of a wood-louse and she settled for a pancake with jam running off the edges. They didn't have to be live things.

The muffled thud of the back door closing made her eyes dart to the door before her and the shuffling of padded feet. Padded? Was it May Thomson, their slippered, old spinster neighbour, ready to throw their key onto the ground so that she could insert her own? Maggie smiled with the hope of catching her out, of sitting mute throughout the performance, until May's own key failed to turn the lock and the realisation dawned that someone was in occupation. Not that she'd apologise, or pick up the thrown key and return it to the lock: that would be too much like admitting her mistake.

Maggie sat perfectly still in the silence. The person was standing there, waiting. For her? Had some man guessed at her presence and was aiming to grab her and drag her off to the dark depths of the air-raid shelter? Fear made her bowels convulse and she gasped and held a groan in her throat. But the splash was a give-away and she would have to get some paper from the rattling holder, too far above her and to her left for care. She could see herself reaching with both hands, toppling from her throne to bash her head off the brick wall. Why did they have to fix things out of reach to kids?

She listened: there should be breathing. If he was standing in the recess of the door, she would hear him. There was no one there, couldn't be anyone. She began to sing, quietly at first, then louder, till the crescendo of "Come All Ye Faithful" was shattering the still air:
"Glo-oh-oh-oh-oh-oh, Glo-oh-oh-oh-oh, Glo-oh-oh-oh-oh-oh, Glo-oh-oh-oh-oh-oh . . ."; she stood up, arranged her clothing and yanked the chain with a skip to one side, away from any drop of water which might leap out and land on her head.
"Hosanna in excelsis." The roar from the cistern drowned her words as she wrenched the door wide on twilight. Nothing. The back door open, she raced down the lobby, searching in vain for the strip of light at May's door which would convince her that May had been on a recce.

"You haven't been in there all this time . . .?" Her mother, at the cooker, threw the question over her shoulder at Maggie.

41

"Not because I like it," replied Maggie, flopping next to Tommy on the settee, where she picked up a newspaper. "I nearly had a fight with May, but she must have seen our key and changed her mind."

"She hit me," said Tommy.

"No," said their mother.

"She did so. Yesterday, before you came home. She clattered me over the knuckles with a clothes peg, one of those big, fat ones."

"Well she must have had a good reason," their mother countered. "Were you kicking the ball near her window again?"

"No I wasn't. Me and Jimmy were in the back fixing my bike and when we came in the lobby she said 'Was it you knocking on my door?' and then she hit me and it was sore."

"And was it you?" asked Maggie.

"I've just told you. We were out in the back."

"She could be better named," said their mother, setting the table. "I mean, if they'd called her January . . ."

Maggie looked at Tommy for a sign that he's understood their mother's words: but he responded to the unspoken question by placing a finger at his temple and wiggling it.

"Are you sure it was her?" their mother asked Maggie. "I haven't clapped eyes on her all day. And there's no sound from her wireless. Tommy, go out the back and see if her light's on."

"Oh Mum. . . ."

"Go on."

Tommy returned within seconds:

"No."

"Did you look?"

"Yeeees."

"Where could she be?" asked Maggie.

"Oh visiting her sister or something. I'll listen for her coming home after you two are in bed."

Maggie turned to object. May never went further than the corner shop; but there was a certainty in her mother's face which stopped her. She shrugged and turned instead to the daily cartoon.

They had lived for so long across the main lobby from May, from the time when Maggie was a baby, that Maggie never questioned her nature, took the bad temper for granted. Only once had she wondered why this old woman held onto her privacy so tightly and that was when Maggie had run messages for her during the last 'flu epidemic. Without actually expecting to get across May's threshold, since nobody, even at New Year, went into anyone else's small space in the tenements, Maggie had nonetheless been surprised and impressed at the lengths to which May had gone to keep her messenger out.

Each morning, Maggie would find a list of groceries just inside the ailing May's door and on her return from the corner shop, would leave the message-bag in the place where the list had been. Maggie knew then what a tremendous effort May had made to get the list to its resting-place, because Maggie had only recently recovered

42

from the 'flu herself and had been incapable of the smallest head movement for days. Even turning her eyes to her Mother's face at the side of her bed had exhausted her.

On the morning when no list had been there, she had tapped lightly on the inside, living-room door, which edged open an inch with the impact.

"That's far enough!" May's brusque voice had called.

"Oh, are you better now?" Maggie had replied to the invisible May. May had made a coughing sound and Maggie wondered if it was meant as a laugh.

"You needn't come back," May then said and Maggie had closed her front door quietly, feeling something like shame.

"Don't pay any attention," her mother said, when Maggie complained about May's treatment of her. "She's grateful to you in her own way."

Within days, the old relationship had been reestablished and Maggie had done her best to avoid their closest neighbour, crossing paths with her only at the door of their shared outside toilet, in a silence which Maggie sensed was full of anger on May's side. And then the anger went.

"Come on. Bed," her mother said and Maggie laughed at Tommy's objections: they both knew there was nothing of interest on the radio at that rime of night.

In the morning, Maggie was wakened by her mother shaking her shoulder: "Maggie. Maggie, I'm worried about May. She didn't come in last night. That makes two days since I last saw her. I think something's happened to her." Her mother's anxious whispering brought Maggie's eyes wide in the half-light.

"Eh? But what can we do?"

"Ssh, you'll waken Tommy." Tommy stirred in the next bed, but said nothing.

"Get dressed, quickly. You'll have to climb in her window."

"But what if she's OK? She'll kill me."

"I'll explain. Come on, hurry."

In the back garden, shivering, her face pressed to the glass of May's living-room window, Maggie could barely make out shapes:

"I can't see a thing."

"Move over." Her mother, full-stretch, forced the upper part of the window frame up, the screen moving with it, then pulled on the gap, widening it. She ducked her head, then said quickly:

"Maggie, she's half in, half out of the bed. I don't think she can move. You'll have to climb in and open the door for me."

Her mother pushing, Maggie hauling on the taps, she managed to squirm across the sink and drop onto the floor. She saw May then, head and shoulders supported by the high bed, her legs bent, feet on the floor, the nightdress rucked up across her belly.

"Are you OK, Ma . . ., Miss Thomson?" Maggie approached, peering, keeping her eyes on May's face. She knew the lay-out of the room instinctively: it was exactly like their own. But the few pieces of furniture made the space seem vast, the high ceiling a vault. Maggie realised that she had been whispering, so she said again:

"Are you OK?" though the question seemed pointless until a rattle began in May's throat:

"Ugggrrr," she said and the tip of her tongue rolled across the left side of her lower lip.

It was an angry, ugly sound, a warning to Maggie for daring to enter. She looked down at May's useless hands which hung inches from the floor on either side of her and said:

"I'll just go and get my mum."

Standing over her, Maggie reached for the folds of nightdress determined to cover her before anyone else came in. When her hand accidentally touched the cold flesh of May's stomach, she glanced down in alarm and saw May's sparse brush:

"You're freezing," she said.

May's eyes followed Maggie's, her mouth immobile. Without spectacles, the face seemed naked too. Maggie turned and stumbled past the kitchen table, to the front door and her mother's explanation. Nobody would convince her that May felt gratitude.

Rosemary Mackay

While everyone around her has sweated and cursed from days of constant carting and carrying, she has stolen time for herself. She has laid her Bible open on the well scrubbed table and heaped a few handfuls of meal beside it. So, she has honoured equally the superstitions of all her generations.

She has tidied the box bed, where her bairn was born and set the bolster straight, leaving a stray dark hair between the folds of the sheet. She has absorbed the details of the small room, imprinting them on her memory for all time. A clock, ticking loudly in the empty room, its brass pendulum swinging prettily through the curling patterns on the glass. The fire, shifting slightly, and the ash trickling softly through the embers. A blue fly, buzzing crazily against the small window, seeking the outside air hopelessly. The thick gold autumn sunlight, striping the uneven floor in patterns of light and shade. She has stored this knowledge for her son.

She has chosen to take with her only what can be carried in a plaid, though others have taken everything, in hope. She has closed the door for the last time. She has not wept.

Now the sea wrenches her and the boats away from the shore, the rowers straining in their rough grey shirts towards the sturdy black steamship. She looks steadily to her house through every swell and drop, mindless even of the bairn whining with fright in her skirts. In moments when the house is torn from her sight by the swell, a terror grips her, showing only in the whitening of her grip on the gunwale.

On the deck of the steamship she prays silently into a dancing wind, until the bold rocks of her island home dwindle to a haze and are lost to sight. Then at last she turns away and her bairn nestles quickly into the fold of her arm. Her hand comes to rest on his dark head. Her man looks at her face and turns quickly away to look out over the sea. She is beyond comfort. Even the familiar faces of her neighbours, solemn or bowed from sight, do not move her or stir her pity for their common plight.

While, in the alien land, she unpacks memory from the rough tweed plaid, a fulmar is roosting undisturbed on the roof of her old home. The turf is already white from his occupation. While she helps her son to tie the laces of his new strong boots, in the cracks of that flagstone path, coarse nettle seedlings root and flourish, untrodden. While she scrubs and cleans the house with stairs, spiders are lacing up every corner of that room and baby mice curl warmly in the mattress straw. While her man learns to plant ever more trees, her sea-born spirit is netted by their green shadows in a land of close horizons.

Her mind, tuned to one song, will never learn another. She will wake every morning in a confusion of new geometry, with the old room firmly in her eyes. Stories of the homeland will begin to ring in her son's ears like warning bells, threatening and challenging his right to games and careless laughter, warping his love for her.

There will be no more yielding softness in her. Her man will dwindle and fail under her cold stare and hate will grow where love had been before. She will look on many births and many funerals, unmoved. She will see her son embrace a stranger bride and leave her, alone, in the house with stairs, where even from the highest window she cannot see the sea.

And through her seasons among the strangers, winter storms will rip at the turf cladding of her old home and expose the bones of many dogs along the beaches. Shipwrecked sailors will roll tobacco in the pages of her Bible and rest briefly on her bed, cursing their own fate but heedless of hers. One stone, and then another, will fall with sudden thunder on to the flags, startling gulls into frenzied protest. Meadow grass will soften the contours of the graves, but whistling winds will make stark angles in the glass and masonry. A ewe will give birth in the shelter of the crumbling walls, her lamb steaming in the winter air. But still the woman will go on polishing the memory of her home, to keep it shining like new in her mind's eye.

With time, her hands will twist and warp and rest useless in her lap. She will die, alone and with little dignity, willing her ghost to take the journey home, in defiance of all the teachings of her faith. There will be no-one there to mourn her on that day. She will be buried among the strangers.

At last the strangers will revive interest in the evacuation. Some will make the journey and seek out the curious place. Two of her grandchildren will sit in awe among the stones of the ruined shells of homes and wonder at the lives the old ones lived out there. One will be hypnotised by the peace and embrace a grand nostalgia. The one who looks so much like her grandmother will grasp generations of history in a moment and be filled with impotent, but enduring, rage.

Wilma Murray

46

That, kiddo, was called a contraction. No doubt about it now.

So. This is it, then.

It's just you and me now. Till birth us do part.

Don't get scared. I reckon we have a few hours left to ourselves before we have to tell anyone. And I need the time. Okay? You see, while the world is turning ever so casually on its axis, I am about to be slipped into a supporting role for the rest of my life to leave you the centre stage. It may be the first day of your life, but it's the last day of my childhood. So give me a few hours to get used to the idea, eh?

That sounds selfish. I know. But don't fret, kiddo. There'll be years and years ahead for me to worry about you.

I must say you haven't got much of a day for it. In fact, if I were at all superstitious and chose to believe the omens like grandma did, I can tell you they're not good. The sun's not even shining. There's a distinct smell of withering in the air this grey September morning. See, the roses are rotted with the rain and it looks like every pest in the book is busy chewing holes and spitting green. At least Fat-Cat's pleased. They've cut the barley and all the refugee mice have taken him completely by surprise this morning. He'll come in and present us with another little furry body in some advanced state of shock any time now. Stay where you are for a while. Have a last swim around in the warm dark. There's nothing out here for you today. No star in the east or three wise men for you, kiddo.

Funny how I thought I'd be ready for all this. Just a few more hours. Please? If you don't panic, I won't. But it's not how it was described in the manual.

Aww . . . Jesus! Okay, okay. I'll see if I can get you one wise woman.

I told you. The world out here's not a place to rush into. There's AIDS, drugs and God knows what all lurking out here, colds and rotten teeth, acid rain and nuclear waste - all this in spite of the wonder of the modern world. (They can predict the return of Halley's comet with pin-point accuracy, but they couldn't tell me when you would be born. Doesn't that seem odd to you?)

What else can I tell you about your chosen birth day, then? Well, Nelson Mandela is *still* in prison, there are killings in Northern Ireland, wars in three continents, famine in another, but, Coronation Street carries on. Women are spying on Greenham Common and picking brambles at the same time, pinning hopes on wholesome pies and laying down a future in jams and good strong wine. Just wait till you taste a bramble and apple pie, kiddo!

It's a funny old world. And don't you go expecting me to explain it all away, either. I'll wipe your bum and put plasters on your knees, maybe teach you to play the piano and help you with your homework., After that, you're on your own, kiddo. Like the rest of us. Mummies can't kiss the world better any more and there ain't no fairy godmothers.

There are grandmas, though. They're the next best thing. They're good with the fairy tales, are grandmas. I have one of my own, so I know. Of course, you'll be seeing her soon. She's something else, that one. When I asked her - you know, woman to woman for the very first time - what it was like the day mother was born, she told me it was snowing! The omens seemed good for the times, she said. It was

Winston Churchill's birthday and St Andrew's day, so the flags were flying. Well, you had to keep your spirits up during the war, she said. She would tell my mother the flags were up for her and not worry her about things like war.

You could keep them ignorant then, you see, kiddo. No TV, see. Anyway, she told me all of that, almost in one breath, but did not volunteer one word about the birth itself. She remembers the midwife's jokes and her bad feet, though. She patted my arm finally and said I'd forget about it as soon as it was over. That was a great help. And mother, she still can't bear to watch war documentaries or read about the Holocaust because she knows she spent the whole sorry six years skipping through other people's time. I teased her about grandma telling her the flags were for her and she gave me that look. The one that can tidy up a room.

Not that she was any great help either. When I asked her what it was like the day I was born, she said it was a scorcher and she just about died of thirst. My god! I should have thought that was the least of her problems. I persisted, but it's not easy asking your mother little questions like - how was your labour? She told me it took twenty-eight hours and the temperature outside rose to eighty at one point. Some kids at the local school sports collapsed with heat stroke, she remembers. I wasn't asking about the weather, dammit.

If you're a girl, I promise, I do, I promise that when the time comes I'll tell you every last detail. Come to think of it, I'll tell you even if you're a boy. I'm all for equality, kiddo.

In the end, she confided it wasn't too bad. Anyway, she said, it'll all be worth it. And that's it. That's the extent of the experience handed down through the generations to me, now, with my big belly.

Hey! Is this hurting you as much as it's hurting me? Read the book, kiddo. This is supposed to be the good bit. So hang on to your hat, because here it comes again.

Holy. Hell!

I knew it. I just knew it. She was lying through her teeth. Twenty-eight hours she was in labour with me. Twenty-eight hours! And all she'll tell me is that it wasn't too bad. So what's bad? What are we registering on the Richter scale now, for example? I tell you, this is getting scary.

Where's that book?

Where's that bloody book?

Recite something, the book says. Quick.

> Humpty Dumpty sat on a wall
> Humpty Dumpty had a great fall
> All the King's horses
> And all the King's men
> Couldn't put Humpty together again.

That's going to go down well in the ambulance. Speaking of which, I'm going to phone them. Sorry, kiddo, but I'm losing my grip, as they say, and it's your fault.

No, forgive me. That's not true. It's their fault. The secret society of mothers out there.

You okay in there? Just hold on a while yet, kiddo. Hey! I'll soon have to stop calling you that. You'll have a name. And all the other trappings of a statistic. They'll start a file on you and you'll get orange juice, an education and free dental treatment till you're sixteen. Then you'll get to collect Social Security like the rest of us. Just like your Dad. And if you're wondering where your other parent is at this critical juncture in your life, he's out looking for work, again. That's where he is. I sent him off this morning without telling him about the queer ache in my back that started all this. Well, he would only have fussed. He's a lovely man, though. You'll like him. I promise. But, if he doesn't find a job soon, you'll have that on your birth certificate, you know. Father - Unemployed.

This is not funny any more. I'm not sure I can take much more of it. WHY DIDN'T SOMEBODY TELL ME?

> Humpty Dumpty sat on a wall
> Humpty Dumpty had a great fall . . .

Myself, I think he was conned. Just like me. Why else would an egg go and jump off a wall? Well, there's a lot of it about, I suppose. Conspiracy, that is. I did warn you it wasn't much of a world. Everybody's at it. Governments, drug companies, slimming magazines and that silly bitch who ran the Ante-Natal classes. To think I believed all that guff about clenched fists mimicking contractions.

Remember? 'Tighten. Clench. Ho-o-ld it. Re-lax.' What a load of crap.

Just like mother and her 'not too bad'. Just like all of them, all the bloody mothers down all the bloody generations who have never told it as it is. THANK YOU FOR NOTHING ALL YOU MOTHERS OUT THERE.

Oh, but it will all be worth it, they say.

Oh? Will it really?

You'll forget about it as soon as it's over, they say.

No I won't. I'm going to spill the beans. I'm going to tell all. And I'm telling you, kiddo. This is hell.

This. This is the biggest con of them all. This is the lulu. This . . . Oh, god . . . I bet if someone asked the Virgin Mary what it was like the day Jesus was born, she'd say it was a fine clear night with plenty of stars.

I wonder if Jesus had a birth certificate? Father - God. Hah! Imagine trying to get that through the system today.

INPUT ERROR.

PLEASE RETYPE.

Don't worry, kiddo. You don't have a God in the family. You won't upset any of their computer programs.

> Humpty Dumpty sat on a wall
> Humpty Dumpty had a great fall
> All the King's horses and all the King's men
> Couldn't put Humpty together again.

It has not escaped my notice, kiddo, how much I resemble an egg.

So.

It's time to go, kiddo.

Let's go jump off the wall.

Wilma Murray

# WIDOWS' WALK

She drives with a mind dislocated from all normality by a grief still raw and dangerous. Heedless of her destination she homes in only on the tang of the sea carried westwards on the soft night wind. Some instinct is whipping her towards the enemy she must face at once or live to dread forever.

She has plucked an old ganzie from his chair by the fire and pulled it on over her clothes. It smells of him and boats and the sea. It is comforting, warm and painfully familiar, stirring a riot of memories in her head. In panic, she strains after even the slightest of them in fear that it might slip away from her and be lost. Memories have a new status on this dark summer morning.

The new day comes to mock her. It dawns sweet and clear with a promise of heat. The horizon lightens to the colour of primroses and the dome of the sky is banded with delicate glassy blues beyond the reach of any artist. The air is crystal she could ring with a flick of her nail. She sees it, but cannot feel.

The sea when she reaches it is a shimmering blanket. With practised eyes she sees boats, other boats, on their homeward journey, tiny elusive flecks on a great silvered sheet. The nearest one trails gulls in its wake. The catch is coming in. She matches its progress from the shore road seeing, from remembered words, a crew, some asleep below, some on deck gutting with the automatic rhythms of weariness, faces puffy with sleeplessness, hands stung numb while the blade still flashes. The noise and smell are with her, too, mixing with memory in her head to become more real than the wheel she grips.

She heads, with the boat, to port, to a harbour already alive and raucous with the sound of commerce. Today the boat Margaret will not be there. She is drawn, in spite of that, to any homecoming, to see a day he will not see in a place he might have known.

The market is tainted with the din of normality which makes her want to turn and run. She resists, but jumps at every shout and is frozen in her nervousness by the honest stares. She prowls the quayside searching for a sign of him. She sees him in every bearded face, every laughing voice. In the mixture of accents her ear is tuned to pick up only his special cadences.

Fish lie bloody and mutilated at her feet in boxes by the thousand yet there is no smell of slaughter. The ugliness of some she has never seen before tip her into a nightmare world. She steadies herself on a pillar waiting for the overwhelming weakness to pass.

Concern and curiosity are mixed in the faces of the porters. One of them offers her a monkfish tail for her supper and she declines graciously without finding words. It is her first human contact of the day and the normality of it steadies her a little. Then another porter lifts an eel from a box and flaunts it at her with harmless obscenity, as a joke. She turns away, sickened, and sees plundering gulls squabbling for scraps of guts in the foul, oily harbour. She escapes through a slick of crushed ice, blood and scales. There is no connection with him here, no comfort in his world of men untouched, even excited, by this killing trade.

Outside the market she slows to a walk and on and away from the horror of the market, oblivious to the sun in her eyes. She comes at last to a quiet place where the springy turf relays no football and there is nothing but the cry of birds and the slap of the sea. She rests a while, searching for some calming thought but each rock below her becomes a body and the sea becomes a huge transparent grave of rotting hulls. The sudden wailing in her ears is a song the sea has made her sing. It is the oldest song on earth. It curses heaven.

'Go back now.' The voice of the woman beside her is gentle and the touch on her arm is soft. Yet it startles her.

'Where am I?' she asks.

'This is Widows' Walk. And see. They are coming.'

From north and south, from all around, they are coming, in twos and threes, a host of women in black. They come to stand beside her, old twisted women in shawls and caps; young women in the first glow of womanhood; women with brave faces; women weeping. Each one comes to touch her gently then steps away. It is a communion. It is an initiation. They sing with her then the song the sea has made her sing, a keening song, a hymn of sorrow. They sing and then they go, quietly, as they came.

She stands alone for a few moments longer looking out over the sea. She is calm now and in touch again. She can feel the spiky grass against her ankles and a whisper of wind on her face. She notices the sea-pinks a little burned by the spray and fat young gulls on ledges of the cliff, rounded and fluffy unlike their streamlined parents. She cannot explain what has happened to her on this clifftop but she knows that something wild has gone out of her with the song the widows sang.

'My man is dead.'

She takes the Widows' Walk back to the town, straining to recall the events that took her there. They come to her only in fragments like glimpses of a fevered dream. She only knows the widows' hands have laid the first healing touch on her, for she feels in some strange way blessed.

Wilma Murray

# THE ROAD TO BERNERA

I drive and she talks. Prattles, babbles, rabbits. I have no time to find the exact word, for the road out of Stornoway has become a crazy roller coaster, tipping up to meet the sky, conjuring lambs and lorries out of hidden dips, setting my teeth in a firm clamp and dislocating my heart.

'. . . so excited . . .'

'Just think . . .'

Snippets of her commentary penetrate my determined concentration.

'Look!' She points so suddenly that I brake in reaction. Her attention has been caught, but not silently, by the peat cutters. Today is a May day and the dun bogs are sprinkled with a gay confetti of anoraks and fertiliser bags. The scarred peat banks are bleeding everywhere from fresh black wounds and the air holds picnic heat.

'. . . afraid it would have changed. My grandmother . . . special tools, you know. She told me . . .'

I am seeing in shades of brown. Brown on green, brown on grey, brown on rust, brown on black. It is subtle colour, the sere disguising brown shading wet black squelch. The crop of the high moor is stone.

She is mouthing in a mind-sleep her romantic dream of brave peasant ancestry again and I refuse to be in collusion with her.

'See all the new white houses?' I choose my words carefully while she searches the townships in vain for old blackhouses.

'And the lambs. Aren't they sweet?'

'Sweet tasting, yes.'

'You're rotten. You know that?'

The lambs rise nervously from their mothers' sides as the car approaches. They are, however, less nervous of me than I am of them. They check with their complacent mothers for alarm signals. Finding none, they sit down again. They are learning to accept the modern world. She is not.

She is quieter while her dream is spoiling, yet she insists it will still be there intact in Bernera, blackhouses and all.

'He was famous, you know. One of the Bernera rioters.'

I have heard this story of the Bernera crofters' resistance against eviction from her so many times now. I do not need to listen, except to her attitudes.

'That was over a century ago. This is now. Look at it!'

'I know. Everything looks so . . . so new.'

She is clearly disappointed with what she is seeing. Only the peat cutters have fitted her picture so far, and they call a spade a taraisgear.

'How do they make a living? How could anyone make a living from land like this?'

'A hidden economy. A job here, a boat there, a loom somewhere else. Bits and pieces, adding up.'

'No wonder grandfather left.'

'Ah, now . . . That's strange, isn't it? Only a generation before that they were risking prison just to stay put.'

She is silent for a few miles. I can almost see her mood turn sour, but I cannot study her face, for the eccentricities of the road are still holding my eyes glued to the windscreen. We pass a tiny school with pupils, at least ten of them, playing on the grass. One car, one teacher. I hope for their sake she is good, for it is a seven year gamble. A boy shoos a cow out of the playground and shuts it out on the road. His actions have a practised confidence, not childlike at all. I realise it is the first cow we have seen, although we have crossed several cattle grids, signposted as such.

'Do you think the house will still be standing?' She is back with her dream, but the shining edges of her certainty have been eroded.

'No. Why should it be?'

'I suppose it's progress.'

We are closer to Bernera now and the land has changed around us. The road is even more devious, the land bare and rock strewn. Cuttings reveal schists contorted in the frozen agony of metamorphosis, the mica glinting in the sun. Elsewhere, the gneiss pushes through in a thousand bald patches, lumpy formless outcrops which defy pattern or symmetry.

'The oldest rocks in the world, you know.' My world of rocks leaks into hers for a moment and she looks around her, without interest.

'Terrible.' She will not comment further.

We can see the island only in quick glimpses as the road twists and slews towards the sea.

'There's a bridge!'

'Of course there is. You don't imagine they still row across like the sherrif's officer did, do you?'

'I never thought. Cars now, of course.'

'As you said. Progress.'

The island has no special magic. It is simply a fragment of the landscape we have been passing through. We stop at the signpost which greets us with FAILTE GU EILEAN BHEARNARAIDH, which even I can translate. This is a foreign land, it tells me.

I feel, irrationally, that we are being watched, that our approach has been monitored, but there is no-one in sight. Then I realise that I have carried across the bridge with me the half registered image of standing stones staring like frozen men from the skyline.

She pulls out her map, the tattered notes, the old photographs collected from wide flung sources over the years. For a moment I envy her quest. Her first excitement has, however, died in her and I find her almost wary. Now that she is so near, she is holding back. Her dream has been shifted into the higher gear of consciousness reality makes us ride.

'Where to, then?'

'Breaclete.'

We drive on through more cattle grids and see no more cattle.

'It's not much to fight over when you see it, is it?' She sighs. 'Would you choose to live here? Would you?'

'No. But I doubt if that's the point. I wasn't born to it. You would have to be, I think.'

The hostile landscape has begun to attract me in a way I am struggling to explain. We are driving over the planet's foundation stones. I, too, might be moved to fight for the right to hold on to a piece of it for posterity. A life-span, the world's problems, even ancestry is set in perspective by a time line that stretches back to the beginning of time on earth.

'How do they bury people here?' My question is innocent, but she turns on me furiously.

'Why do you try to spoil it for me? Ever since we got off the plane in Stornoway and into this car, you have been trying to sabotage my feelings. That remark about the lamb, for a start.'

'Oh, now . . . I was just trying to make you see that what you have been holding in your head about this place is a myth, long gone.'

'Maybe so.' She waves her papers at me. 'But this is no myth. These were my people. What my great-grandfather and others did here broke the pattern of evictions in the rest of the country. They defied the landowners and they won. You can't change that, or belittle it, either. That was not a myth.'

She is right and it is my turn for silence. I admit my admiration for these men and my envy, knowing so little of my own forebears.

We drive towards Breaclete in silence. The straggling township offers us little. The old houses, as elsewhere have been replaced by neat modern dwelling houses, their cement colours not of the land and contrasting strongly with it. We stop at the War Memorial.

'Look at the names. The same names. Macleod, Macauley. The same townships. Tobson, Breaclete, Hacklete. One of these John Macleods must be my uncle John. He died in France.'

'So your family won one fight and lost another.'

She gives me a warning look, but I am in sympathy with her at last. 'At least they understood what they were fighting for in 1874.'

'I don't see any signs of a graveyard, do you?'

'We will have to ask.'

The woman on the road is dressed for winter on this fine May day. 'Bosta,' she says and points along the road. She shows neither surprise or interest at my question.

'You should have told her who you were, what you were looking for. Maybe she could have put you on to somebody.'

She looks sad. 'I couldn't. I would have felt stupid. She seemed so private.'

'But the Bernera riots are history. They even threatened to bring in troops to quell them, didn't they?'

'Oh, yes. But I'm not sure that gives me the right to plunder living memory. Being here, seeing it, it's enough.'

'But your great-grandfather? Dont you . . .?'

'I don't want to know. This is enough.'

'But why?'

'It scares me, this place. Let's go to Bosta.'

The graveyard is miles away from the township, the journey there longer than any I have taken before, except in the largest of cities. On a sharp corner we pass an old man walking very slowly with a stick. I smile a greeting as we pass. He does not smile back. Turning the corner, we are suddenly faced with a desperate gradient and I am totally unprepared for it. The car stutters and dies on the hill. I pull on the handbrake sharply.

'We're going backwards! Do something!'

'The handbrake isn't holding!' Panicky, I manage to get the car to hold on the hill.

'Now what?'

We sit there while I ponder the problem. Directly behind and below us at the foot of the hill is the wall of a house. It is the old man's house, for he stands now watching us from his gate.

'We will just have to roll back down again.'

'But you could hit the wall.'

'Well, we can't go up. The car can't take the hill from here anyway. We'd need a run at it first, from back round that corner. And I'll tell you something else. We have no alternative but to come back up again. There's absolutely no way to turn down there. The road's not much wider than the car.'

The utter absurdity of our situation is somehow increased by the old man's stare. I catch myself blushing. At the same time, there is an element of farce in it.

'What if this was a hearse?'

'That's not funny!' But she laughs, anyway. We both do.

After two tries when we almost leave the road altogether, I make it to the corner safely and get a run at the hill. This time, the car makes it and we stop, in relief, on the tiny summit and look back to see the old man turning into his house.

'Well, that's the show over. I do feel silly.'

In front of us now there is a gate across the road. Here at last are the cattle.

'I wish I'd never come.' She does not make the destination clear, but I suspect she means the entire trip.

'Well, we have to go forward now, whether we like it or not. There's still nowhere to turn.'

The area round the graveyard gives us our only decent opportunity to turn the car safely. We turn and stop, but she will not leave the car. We sit in silence and I cannot reach her as she looks over at the graveyard.

'I don't belong here,' she says at last. 'I wouldn't have the courage to follow a hearse all the way here to bury someone I loved in the sand, on a beach.'

She puts her papers and bits and pieces back in her bag. 'I don't even speak the language.'

She looks once more over at the graveyard and then turns to me. 'Please let's go back now. I want to get out of this place.'

So Bernera sends us scuttling away. As we cross back over the bridge, she takes one last look back and sighs. It is a sigh of relief.

'The rot must have set in with my grandfather in our branch of the family.'

She is very quiet all the way back to Stornoway.

Wilma Murray

# THE KITE

The little plane bumped, lurched and skidded its way across the soft rutted field towards a square patch of tarmac and a red shed which was all that marked out the island airstrip. The wheels spat up gobbets of mud and worse, leaving them in disgusting long-tailed streaks across the windows. Carrie felt a silly but almost irresistible urge to duck. What with that and the scream of the engines, her arrival was a happening registered in her gut if not in her head.

'Damn you, mother! Damn you!' It was a silent chant and not without guilt.

Within seconds, the wind had ripped style and dignity from her practised grasp. She brushed irritably at a mud stain her briefcase had just made on the skirt of her pale suit and searched the faces of the people at the wire barrier for her mother's friend Grace.

A small woman in rubber boots and a hooded duffle coat stepped beyond the barrier and came towards her.

'Carrie?'

'Yes.' They searched each others' faces, but did not touch. That was the way.

'I would hardly have recognised you,' Grace said, picking up two bags and leaving Carrie to follow with the rest.

The van was a wreck, a caricature of a vehicle in the last stages of collapse. Grace drove it without apology, but with multiple muttered oaths.

'You'll come to the farm for dinner, first?'

'Well, if you don't mind, I'd just as soon go straight to the house. I hardly ever eat lunch, anyway. But thanks. And for the lift.'

'Oh, I'm not doing it all for you.'

'I know.'

Carrie turned away to study the subtle green landscape. It was uncomfortably familiar, as though it had lived on in her memory without consent all these years. At the crossroads above the village bay, she had a vivid flashing picture of pedalling furiously against the rain, her skin stung red, her hair plastered across her face. Passing the little village hall, she heard in strong recall the hectic music and felt the slippery floor where she had learned to dance, mostly by watching the others, too shy to risk getting it wrong, except when Magnus was there. These were treacherously happy memories, denying her now the scorn she had needed to feel for the place while she was still safely remote from it.

'What's it like, then, this place of yours?' Gavin had asked when she told him about her mother's will.

'It's not my place.'

'It is now. The house, anyway.'

'It's nothing much. It's at the back of beyond. And the house is a run-down old dump of a place.'

'So what makes you think you can sell it?'

'Oh, it'll sell all right. There are plenty more idiots where mother came from. You know, she dragged us up there every bloody summer after father left us.'

'I know. You've told me. Often.'

'She should have left it to Richard and his brats. Her little blue-eyed boy. He

56

would have preserved it as the family retreat. Oh, why the hell did the devious old bitch leave it to me?'

'For the money?'

'Oh no. Nothing as simple as that! This is a legacy with malice aforethought, that's what this is. And she'll have done a great PR job on me there, with Grace and Magnus and everybody.'

'Who's Magnus?'

'Grace's son. The kid I played with in the holidays. Grew up together, really. Only . . . Only, when I was sixteen, we grew up a little bit too fast for everybody's liking.'

Gavin chuckled. 'You mean sex?'

'Yes. First time, too.' She laughed. 'Only, he fell off a ladder that same afternoon and broke his leg. He had a limp for ages. The proverbial bolt of lightning you know? Put me off sex for a long time, I can tell you.'

'And him, I shouldn't wonder. Did your mother know?'

'She certainly suspected. But no, not really. It gave me a sudden new power over her that summer, because she never really was sure.'

'Did you go back?'

'No. That was the last time. Not welcome, see. I took a holiday job the summer after, then I was away at College. She went back with Richard every year and then lately, on her own. We never got on, you know. And I still won't be welcome there.'

'But you will go?'

'Oh, don't worry. I'll bring you the money. I wouldn't go back if it wasn't for that.'

Gavin had scoffed at the idea of her mother's malice, but now, here in the van, Grace's hostility had confirmed that she still was not welcome here.

'By the way, your first two customers arrive to look at the house tomorrow morning.' Grace was helping her to unload her luggage at the end of the road.

'Good. Sooner the better.'

Together and in renewed silence, they carried the bags up the muddy track to the house that no car could tackle. In spite of the time away, this inconvenient trudge up to the house brought with it an excited sense of homecoming and the first sight of the house stirred a whole pot of confusing memories.

'The key.' Grace held the old-fashioned key out to her, then turned quickly to go.

'You won't come in?' Carrie's voice had a thread of panic in it.

'No. I'll send Magnus over later with some things.'

'Thanks.' She called after Grace, but she was already yards away, hands deep in her pockets, her head down against the wind. Carrie knew then that Grace was still mourning her mother, and a childish knot of tears stuck painfully in her throat for a moment.

The house was stripped and bare except for the furniture, the way they had always left it after the long summer holidays. Rugs, cushions, ornaments and bedding had all been carefully stowed away against mice or damp. It was tidy, clean and cold.

'Hello, house!' She shouted the way her mother had always said they should, rationalising by saying it scared the mice. Her voice sounded stupidly loud now in the empty house and she twisted her mouth self-consciously. This was the reflection which looked back at her from the huge dresser mirror from which there had never been any escape in that room.

She walked through the rooms, making a slow tour of inspection, pulling open drawers, opening cupboards, taking the lids off storage drums. And everywhere she looked she found her mother; the painting clothes and old anoraks in the wardrobe, aprons on the pegs in the corridor, sandals and rubber boots by the hearth in her bedroom, home-made wine in the porch cupboard. In her own room, with a sheaf of memories now floating unbound in her head, she lay down on the mattress and looked up at beams that were as familiar as a face, finding easily again those knots and grains which made landmarks in an imaginary landscape, the childish calming contours of an invented world where mothers had never existed.

Around the hatch leading from her bedroom to the loft where Richard had slept, the same bright rim of light was visible, lit by the roof window. She stared at it until it split and multiplied, just as it always had done, then got up wearily to investigate a tall storage box in the corner.

'Good God Almighty!' The box was full of toys, hers and Richard's, half-remembered, half-forgotten toys; dolls, a shell collection, balls, board games, cars and their old kite with half a mile of butcher's string tangled around a piece of broken broom handle. She smiled, remembering the fusses and fights every year. Who had tangled the kite string again? Whose turn was it to sort it out?

She put the toys back, but took the tangled kite string back with her into the living room. She put it on the dresser.

'My turn this year.' She grinned into the mirror. 'Now,' she added, to this confident reflection, 'we have a house to sell.'

Selling was her metier. Up in the clouds in the flight from London she had plundered her memories of the house only for its selling points, working out careful details of atmosphere she could emphasise, changing disadvantages into advantages by turning subtle loops in language. The image she had decided on was 'quaint'.

A pivot for this image was the old range standing cold now and black, greased over as her mother had left it, not as it had always been in her mind's eye, pulsing with heat and bubbling kettles, drying out their sandals and rubber boots, steaming their bath towels dry on the brass rail under the mantleshelf. She suddenly, urgently needed that reality back, to ward off the cold and the uncomfortable prickles of panic.

Yet, only half an hour into her project, the gap between image and reality had threatened to grow wide enough to fall through. She cursed the black beast pouring foul smelling smutty smoke into the room, forcing her outside into the wind to breathe fresh air in great gulps.

'Shut-up!' Her shout startled the laughing gulls off the chimney ledges.

'Work it out. Work it out.' A familiar old voice chanted in her head.

'Damn you!' She turned back into the house to poke, coughing, at every flap and hole in the range for something that might control the air intake. Damper. The word floated up as she slid a flanged piece of iron across the inside of the chimney piece. Almost immediately, the threads of smoke curled back on themselves and the fire began to settle and then roar satisfactorily.

'There!' Her grubby face looked triumphantly back at her from the dresser mirror. Then she looked down at her hands and her spoiled suit and more soberly counted the cost of this small victory.

'You're a bloody fool!'

She saw and heard the tractor and trailer make its ragged progress up to the house while she was still getting cleaned up. Magnus? She hurried into clean clothes and tried desperately to organise her face in time to greet him. Even so, he took her by surprise, a tall man in dirty dungarees, filling the living room doorway. She stared hard till a boy's face meshed with the one she looked at now.

'Did you knock?'

'Should I have?'

'Well . . . I could have been . . .'

'Oh, come off it! I've seen you in your knickers before now.' He grinned widely, in the old way, and she reddened, her carefully rehearsed expression in ruins. Teasing was no longer part of her repertoire of social transactions. She was badly out of practice.

'What's in the trailer?' She turned to the window, changing the subject.

'A bike, among other things.'

'A bike? What for?'

'Well, unless you've parked the Rolls round the back, it's a long walk to the shop.'

'Oh, I see. Thanks.'

He looked around the room, up at the beams and down at the bare floor.

'Not much of a place now, is it?'

'It'll look better once the carpet's down and everything.'

'You're really going to sell it, then?'

'And why not? It's mine now. I can do what I like with it.'

'So you can. So you can. You don't need the money, though, do you?'

'Yes I do, as a matter of fact.'

'What for?'

'My business.'

He misunderstood. 'I see. Secrets is it? Ah, well, we all have some of those.' He looked at her steadily, then grinned, a little shyly this time.

Childishly, she wanted to punch him, but instead she pushed roughly past him and went outside. They unloaded the bike, some small packing boxes for her mother's personal belongings and a box of groceries Grace had sent over. They took great care not to touch each other. She saw, as he worked, that he no longer limped. One guilt, at least, could be cancelled.

'I'll see you, then.' He swung easily up into the tractor.

'What did your mother say about me today?'

'Nothing.'

Back in the house, she caught sight of her flushed face in the mirror and thought determinedly of Gavin, back in their London flat, waiting for her return with the money. But for the will, they would have been in France now, together, eating oysters in Brittany. They would have been conspiring together over the new magazine, loving partners in business as well as pleasure, using the precious holiday days to plan Gavin's new venture, making up in ideas what they still lacked in financial backing. Money was why she was here, she reminded herself, not a self-indulgent trip down memory lane. Money. Only the money. For Gavin. Pieces of paper to help launch more pieces of paper in sympathetic circulation round the country.

In a fierce burst of activity, drawing sweat, she started to dress up the rooms with all the furnishings stripped from them and stored away for safety. First the carpets, then cushions, ornaments, pictures, rugs, hangings, seat covers, lamps, linen and books. By the time she had finished and settled down by the fire with a cup of coffee, she was looking at a room transformed. Seen again like this after a space of ten years, she was stunned by the style her mother had created. Every individual object was right for the room and in harmony with every other one. It was a room in her mother's style, without compromise. Looking at it humbled her. She sat in nostalgia's punishing grip, trying to remember why she had ever bothered to try to hate this place. Now that she couldn't, she felt she had lost a weapon, weakening the thrusts of her arguments but freeing her from the guilt of the need to hurt, releasing grief. The tears, when they came at last were for a loss she had only that minute started to understand. She lay back, tired and sad beyond the reach of any words and listened to herself sobbing as if she was on the outside looking in.

She surfaced from her distress, shivery and weak, conceding the first round of some obscure test to her mother. Then straightaway she began to organise, out of habit, the words that would explain her defeat, justifying, rationalising, twisting truth to fit. The words came, but the feeling persisted, gnawing at raw nerves. She shook herself out of the chair.

'Christ!' She splashed her face with cruelly cold water and concentrated on compiling a mental list of activities to blunt the edge of the hurting for a while. Stoke the fire, light the lamps, prepare some food, make up her bed. Outside, it was just on the edge of darkness, with some of her precious hours already lost.

First she investigated the groceries box, with surprisingly hungry interest. Bread, yes, butter, cheese. Enough. Then she found two plump shimmering fresh mackerel staring dully at her from a plastic box. Bread and cheese, nothing. She would eat royally.

The meal was, indeed, very good. The room was warm now, smelling of cooking. And paraffin, a lingering testimony to a nervous struggle with the Tilley lamp which now hissed cheerfully above her head. She sat for a long time thoughtfully by the fire, calm now, but with her fingers working like nervous birds at the hundred tangles in the kite string. When she laid the neat roll back on the dresser at last, she felt an absurd sense of achievement.

'Good girl.' She could hear the voice almost.

She poured another glass of home-made wine and wandered outside with it into moonlit windy darkness. She felt at ease in this silent place, but it was an ease more related to defeat than victory. Looking in at the room she had just left, she saw the lamp hanging from its brass cradle, the range glowing cheerfully, the pictures in their places, the table set for one, the kite string neat at last on the dresser.

She set her glass on the windowsill and went inside, pulled the kite from the toy box and tied the string to it.

The big, strong kite caught the wind and soared, tugging hard at the string, leaping higher and higher, crossing the moon and back again like a black witch.

'It's all right,' she shouted. 'I'm here.'

Her laughter as it pulled her in erratic bursts over the sodden grass was a wild releasing noise in the moonlight, with non-one in the world to hear it.

She let the kite out as far as it could go, until it disappeared in the blackness and until the tug of it grew almost too strong to hold. Then, slowly, she wound it in, carefully wrapping the string round the handle in neat figures of eight, the way her mother had taught her. She picked the wet kite off the grass and turned back to the house. The stream of lamplight made a pool of pure gold in the glass on the windowsill. She lifted it and held in to the window.

'Cheers, house! Here's to you and me!'

She drank the raisin wine, her mind already busy with words of explanation for Gavin. She went inside, shutting the heavy door against the wind.

Wilma Murray

**Three's Company,** chute, from top to bottom:

**Rosemary Mackay,** Aberdonian. Educated in Aberdeen and at Aberdeen University. Twice retired from teaching. Married with two children. Wishes to write more and better in the future. Has just completed a novella.

**Sheena Blackhall** studied at Gray's School of Art, Aberdeen, and is a member of the Aberdeen Artist's Society and a former member of the Forecourt Art Group. She has written, illustrated and published four volumes of poems, (mainly Scots), and one collection of short stories, and has short stories in Original Prints 1 and 2 (Polygon, Scottish Women Writers' Anthology). Other stories (in Scots and English) have appeared in Cencrastus, Edinburgh Review, Chapman, Lallans, and Leopard. Her interests are Belgian Surrealism, Tibetan-meditation-visualisation, and Scots poetry.

**Wilma Murray** was born in Aberdeenshire. Educated in Aberdeen University. Taught for 10 years, now lectures at the Northern College of Education. Took to writing short stories in 1983. Has published in various anthologies and magazines, mostly Scottish. Hopes to achieve her own collection of short stories.